Senegal:

Malaria Operational Plan FY 2014

TABLE OF CONTENTS

ABBREVIATIONS and ACRONYMS

ACT	artemisinin-based combination therapy
ANC	antenatal care
BCC	behavior change communication
CDC	Centers for Disease Control and Prevention
cDHS	Continuous Demographic and Health Survey
CFA	West African Financial Community Franc (USD $1 = F CFA 500)
CMS	Central Medical Stores
DHS	Demographic and Health Survey
DSDOM	*dispensateur de soins à domicile* (village malaria worker)
FY	fiscal year
GHI	Global Health Initiative
Global Fund	Global Fund to Fight AIDS, Tuberculosis and Malaria
HIV/AIDS	human immunodeficiency virus /acquired immunodeficiency syndrome
IEC	information, education, communication
IPTp	intermittent preventive treatment in pregnant women
IRD	*Institut de Recherche pour le Développement*
IRS	indoor residual spraying
ITN	insecticide-treated bed net
LLIN	long-lasting insecticide-treated bed net
LNCM	*Laboratoire national de control des médicaments* (National Drug Control Laboratory)
M&E	monitoring and evaluation
MIP	malaria in pregnancy
MIS	Malaria Indicator Survey
MOH	Ministry of Health
NMCP	National Malaria Control Program
PECADOM	*prise en charge à domicile* (home-based management of malaria)
PMI	President's Malaria Initiative
RDT	rapid diagnostic test
SMC	seasonal malaria chemoprevention
SNEIPS	National Health Education and Information Service
SP	sulfadoxine-pyrimethamine
SP-AQ	sulfadoxine-pyrimethamine/amodiaquine
TA	technical assistance
UC	universal coverage
UCAD	*Université Cheikh Anta Diop*
UNICEF	United Nations Children's Fund
USAID	United States Agency for International Development
USG	United States Government
WHO	World Health Organization

I.   EXECUTIVE SUMMARY

Malaria prevention and control is a major foreign assistance objective of the United States Government (USG). In May 2009, President Barack Obama announced the Global Health Initiative (GHI), a six-year, comprehensive effort to reduce the burden of disease and promote healthy communities and families around the world. Through the GHI, the United States will partner with countries to improve health outcomes, with a particular focus on improving the health of women, newborns, and children.

The President's Malaria Initiative (PMI) is a core component of the GHI, along with human immunodeficiency virus /acquired immunodeficiency syndrome (HIV/AIDS), and tuberculosis. PMI was launched in June 2005 as a five-year, $1.2 billion initiative to rapidly scale up malaria prevention and treatment interventions and reduce malaria-related mortality by 50% in 15 high-burden countries in sub-Saharan Africa. With passage of the 2008 Lantos-Hyde Act, funding for PMI has been extended through fiscal year (FY) 2014 and, as part of the GHI, the goal of PMI has been adjusted to reduce malaria-related mortality by 70% in the original 15 countries by the end of 2015.

Senegal was selected as a PMI country in 2006. Large-scale implementation of malaria control activities began in FY 2007 and progressed rapidly with significant progress demonstrated to date.

This FY 2014 Malaria Operational Plan for Senegal was developed in close consultation with the National Malaria Control Program (NMCP) and with the participation of all national and international partners involved with malaria prevention and control in the country. The activities that PMI is proposing to support with FY 2014 funding fit well with the 2011-2015 National Malaria Control Strategic Plan and build on investments made by PMI and other partners to improve and expand malaria-related interventions over the last five years. This FY 2014 MOP is designed to support the objective set by the Government of Senegal and stakeholders to engage in the malaria pre-elimination phase, as data have demonstrated significantly reduced prevalence in many parts of the country. In line with GHI principles, PMI has reinforced its efforts to build capacity and integrate across programs. The proposed FY 2014 PMI budget for Senegal is $21.6 million, of which 43% will be managed directly by local entities/institutions.

Senegal has a population estimated at 13.2 million in 2014, with approximately 2.2 million children less than five years of age and 528,000 pregnant women. Malaria is still a major cause of morbidity and mortality and a high priority for the government, even though the number of reported cases of malaria has dropped significantly since 2007-2008. While the decline in the first year can be partially ascribed to a change in the malaria case definition that now requires parasitological confirmation of all cases, the proportion of all outpatient visits due to confirmed malaria continued to fall, from 6% in 2008 to 3% in 2009. From July 2010 to March 2013, routine morbidity and mortality data were not available due to a health worker data retention strike. Now that the strike has ended, the Ministry of Health (MOH) is working to catch up with routine data collection for the missing years.

The 2012 continuous Demographic and Health Survey (cDHS) showed that under-five mortality continued to fall, from 121 per 1000 live births in 2005 to 65 in 2012, a 46% drop in seven years. The proportion of households owning at least one insecticide-treated net (ITN) increased from 20% in 2005 to 73% in 2012, and the proportion of children under five sleeping under an ITN the previous night increased from 7% to 46%, with similar trends for pregnant women. The proportion of pregnant women receiving two doses of intermittent preventive treatment with sulfadoxine-pyrimethamine (SP) fell from 52% in 2008 to 39% in 2010, a decline due to many factors including problems in maintaining supplies of the drug. A slight increase was noted in 2012, to 41%.

The following paragraphs summarize progress made during the last 12 months and proposed activities for FY 2014 funding.

Insecticide-Treated Nets (ITNs): During FY 2013, PMI supported the distribution of free and subsidized long-lasting insecticide-treated bed nets (LLINs) nationwide via multiple continuous distribution channels. These include free LLINs to pregnant women attending antenatal care (ANC) clinics and to primary school children and subsidized nets to other health facility clients and through community-based organizations. To promote demand for and correct use of ITNs, PMI has also invested in behavior change communication (BCC) activities using primarily community-based networks.

With FY 2014 funding, PMI and the NMCP plan to continue supporting the routine distribution system to bridge the gap for those that do not possess an LLIN and to replace nets no longer appropriate to be used. PMI plans to procure one million LLINs to support primarily routine distribution strategies, as well as assistance to mass campaign if needed. The total LLIN need for 2015 is estimated at 5.9 million. PMI LLINs will complement those expected to be procured by the NMCP via the Global Fund to Fight AIDS, Tuberculosis and Malaria (Global Fund).

Indoor Residual Spraying (IRS): During FY 2013, PMI supported IRS activities in four districts sprayed in previous years (Koumpentoum, Koungheul, Malem Hodar, and Velingara). Bendiocarb was the selected insecticide, as little resistance had been shown to this insecticide after last year's spray operations. The 2013 spray operations began in July, later than in previous years in order to maximize the effective duration of bendiocarb. A total of 206,704 structures were sprayed (98% of those visited and eligible for spraying) and 690,090 people were protected. With FY 2014 funding, PMI plans to support spray operations and entomological monitoring in the same four districts. An estimated 215,000 structures are expected to be sprayed, protecting more than 1.1 million people. The insecticide choice for 2014 will be an organophosphate.

Malaria in Pregnancy (MIP): The significant drop in coverage for intermittent preventive treatment in pregnant women (IPTp) revealed by the 2010-2011 DHS can be attributed largely to recurrent stock-outs of SP. In FY 2013, PMI continued support for training and supervision to assure that quality services were offered to the extent possible. As the country is expected to procure the stock of SP needed for the foreseeable future, PMI is focusing on integration of new World Health Organization (WHO) recommendations, monitoring and supportive supervision of MIP service delivery, improvement of data collection regarding IPTp, and training of new staff on IPTp, the importance of LLIN use in pregnancy, diagnosis and management of malaria in pregnancy, and counseling and interpersonal communication skills. With FY 2014 funds, PMI plans to continue to support the same activities.

Case Management: Support from PMI for case management in the formal health sector includes training and supportive supervision, using a strategy of peer supervision and mentoring termed *TutoratPlus* in some districts. In FY 2013 PMI supported the training of 277 health workers at the facility level and 800 at the community level on malaria case management including rapid diagnostic tests (RDTs) and artemisinin-based combination therapies (ACTs). The community level program now includes a total of 2,143 health huts and 1,647 sites, as well as 976 village malaria workers. During FY 2013 PMI supported a pilot of integrated case management of pneumonia, diarrhea, and malaria in the home-based program, in which 87 village workers were trained. PMI is also supporting the NMCP to introduce two new WHO recommended interventions: pre referral treatment for severe malaria and seasonal malaria chemoprevention (SMC). The first SMC campaign was implemented in four health districts at the beginning of November, 2013 and covered approximately 53,000 children.

With FY 2014 funding, PMI plans to support the procurement of 2.2 million RDTs, as well as microscopes and laboratory consumables. PMI plans to support training and supervision for RDTs and microscopic diagnosis of malaria, as well as quality control for microscopy. PMI also plans to procure approximately 600,000 ACT treatments and fund training and supportive supervision to maintain quality case management at all levels. PMI plans to continue to procure sulfadoxine-pyrimethamine/amodiaquine (SP-AQ) and support implementation for SMC among children 3-120 months, benefitting approximately 600,000 children. Finally, PMI plans to continue to support pre-referral treatment for severe malaria in an effort to significantly reduce malaria mortality.

Monitoring and Evaluation (M&E)/Operations Research: PMI's M&E activities are carried out jointly with the NMCP and other partners, and PMI supports implementation of the NMCP M&E plan. During FY 2013 the first round of data collection was carried out for the continuous Demographic and Health Survey (cDHS), which provides data on a yearly basis to enable M&E and decision-making for malaria programming and other health interventions. Results were presented to the MOH and partners in September 2013, showing slight improvements over the 2010 DHS.

In response to the growing surveillance needs as Senegal moves towards pre-elimination, PMI's FY 2014 resources are planned to be used to strengthen the national malaria surveillance system, including the integration of weekly case notification, in both the formal public health sector (hospitals, centers, and posts) and at the community level (health huts and home-based management). This support is expected to include electronic transmission of data. Districts where IRS has been withdrawn will be prioritized.

PMI plans to also support other activities aimed at improving the information system and data generation for timely decision making, as well as the cDHS and the evaluation of the 2011-2015 malaria strategic plan.

Behavior Change Communication (BCC): During FY 2013 PMI continued to support community-based communications activities to increase LLIN use, promote prompt care seeking, and encourage acceptance of IRS. Home visits and discussion groups were complemented by mass media approaches, particularly using local language radio stations. Work also began with the National Health Information and Education Service to implement a national BCC framework. The results from two phases of the "Culture of Net Use" study conducted in 2012 were used to inform the design and focus of BCC activities, including a multi-media campaign to promote the use of LLINs.

With FY 2014 funds, PMI plans to support a range of communications activities to influence the social and behavior changes needed to improve the adoption of key malaria prevention and care seeking behaviors (e.g., net ownership, proper net use, net repair, and when and where to seek care).

Health Systems Strengthening and Capacity Building: Since beginning work in Senegal, PMI has supported strengthening of the health system and capacity building of the MOH to implement its malaria control program. Support to improve the supply chain and drug management continued during FY 2013, in close collaboration with the new leadership of the Central Medical Stores (CMS). PMI continued its support to the National Drug Control Laboratory (LNCM) to carry out drug quality monitoring activities. PMI also supported the NMCP to supervise case management at hospitals, health centers, and health posts, and worked to build national capacity for M&E through funding the attendance of health system staff at the annual data management and M&E course.

With FY 2014 funds, PMI plans to support activities to develop capacity at sub-national and central levels to sustain and carry forward the NMCP's progress towards its pre-elimination objective in 2015. Technical assistance (TA) to support and strengthen the pharmaceutical management system is planned to continue. Specific activities include support for program supervision, organization of a malariology course and drug quality monitoring.

II. STRATEGY

1. Introduction

The President's Malaria Initiative (PMI) is a core component of the Global Health Initiative (GHI), along with human immunodeficiency virus /acquired immunodeficiency syndrome (HIV/AIDS) and tuberculosis. PMI was launched in June 2005 as a 5-year, $1.2 billion initiative to rapidly scale up malaria prevention and treatment interventions and reduce malaria-related mortality by 50% in 15 high-burden countries in sub-Saharan Africa. With passage of the 2008 Lantos-Hyde Act, funding for PMI has been extended through fiscal year (FY) 2013 and, as part of the GHI, the goal of PMI has been adjusted to reduce malaria-related mortality by 70% in the original 15 countries by the end of 2015. This will be achieved by reaching 85% coverage of the most vulnerable groups — children under five years of age and pregnant women — with proven preventive and therapeutic interventions, including artemisinin-based combination therapies(ACTs), insecticide-treated nets (ITNs), intermittent preventive treatment of pregnant women (IPTp), and indoor residual spraying (IRS).

Senegal was selected as a PMI country in 2006. Large-scale implementation of ACTs and rapid diagnostic tests (RDTs) began in 2007 and progressed rapidly with support from PMI and other partners. ACTs and IPTp are now being used in all public health facilities nationwide, RDTs are used to confirm malaria cases at all levels of the health system (including the community level) and more than 6 million long-lasting insecticide-treated bed nets (LLINs) have been distributed using a universal coverage (UC) approach since 2010.

This FY 2014 Malaria Operational Plan presents a detailed implementation plan for Senegal, based on the PMI Multi-Year Strategy and Plan and the National Malaria Control Program's (NMCP's) five-year strategy. It was developed in consultation with the NMCP, with participation of national and international partners involved with malaria prevention and control in the country. Proposed activities build on investments made by PMI and other partners to improve and expand malaria-related services, including the Global Fund to Fight AIDS, Tuberculosis, and Malaria (Global Fund) malaria grants. This document briefly reviews the current status of malaria control policies and interventions in Senegal, describes progress to date, identifies challenges and unmet needs if the targets of the NMCP and PMI are to be achieved, and describes planned activities for FY 2014 funding.

2. Malaria Situation in Senegal

Senegal's estimated population in 2014 will be approximately 13.4 million. Although substantial improvements have been achieved since the 1960s, Senegal's indicators of human development remain low, with the country ranked 154 out of 187 countries worldwide on the Human Development Index[1]. The infant mortality rate is 47 and the under-five mortality rate is 72 per 1,000 live births[2]. Maternal mortality is estimated to be 392 per 100,000 live births and the mean life expectancy is 56 years[2]. The adult HIV prevalence rate is estimated at 0.7% for adults 15-49 years of age, with 54,000 adults and 5,000 children estimated to be living with HIV/AIDS[3].

Malaria is endemic throughout Senegal and 100% of the population is at risk of the disease. The three ecological zones, based on annual rainfall, are the northern Sahelian zone with < 300 mm of rainfall occurring between July and September, a central Sahelian zone with 400 – 1000 mm of rainfall occurring between July and October, and a southern tropical zone with 1000 – 1250 mm of rainfall occurring between June and October. The country can also be divided into two epidemiological zones— the tropical, with year-round transmission peaking during the rainy season and the Sahelian, with high transmission toward the end of and immediately after the rainy season and lower transmission during the rest of the year. Transmission in the Sahelian zone may occur throughout the year, often as small outbreaks, in areas close to rivers or other water sources that persist through the dry season. In peri-urban areas, persistent flooding during and after rainy season has led to higher peaks in transmission during the rainy season and a longer transmission season. *Plasmodium falciparum* is the major malaria parasite species, accounting for more than 90% of all infections. The main vector species are *Anopheles gambiae sensu strictu, An. arabiensis, An. funestus,* and *An. melas*. The species distribution depends on rainfall and the presence of permanent sources of water.

The vulnerable groups in Senegal comprise an estimated 2.2 million children under five and 528,000 pregnant women. According to routine data collected by the NMCP, between 2001 and 2006 malaria was responsible for just over one-third of all outpatient consultations. In October 2007, the case definition of malaria changed from a purely clinical definition to one that relies on parasitological confirmation. From that point on, clinicians were directed to test all suspected cases of malaria and to treat and report only those cases with positive results. The proportion of suspected cases tested rose from 15% in January 2008 to 89% in December 2008, and in 2009, 86% of suspected cases were tested.

As a result of these changes, the proportion of all outpatient visits due to malaria fell from 36% (clinically diagnosed) in 2001 to 6% (parasitologically confirmed) in 2008. The proportion of all deaths in children under five in health facilities that were attributed to malaria also fell from 30% to 7% over the same timeframe. Although the change in the case definition of malaria obscured assessment of the impact of program activities, between 2008 and 2009 this reduction continued, with malaria representing only 3% of all outpatient visits and 4% of all deaths in 2009.

Routine morbidity and mortality data were not available between 2010 and 2012 because health worker unions were staging a nationwide data retention strike. Although clinical activities continued, health workers stopped reporting any routinely collected data, including those related to malaria. This data strike was lifted in March 2013, and the process of rebuilding the system and backfilling the data is underway.

3. Country Health System Delivery Structure and Ministry of Health (MOH) Organization

Administratively, the country is divided into 14 regions and 46 departments. The health system functions at the level of the regions (each with a Regional Chief Medical Officer) and is further decentralized into health districts that may be all or part of an administrative department. Health districts are led by the District Chief Medical Officer who, together with the District Health Management Team, oversees care and treatment at the District Health Center and at peripheral facilities throughout the district, as well as overseeing prevention activities.

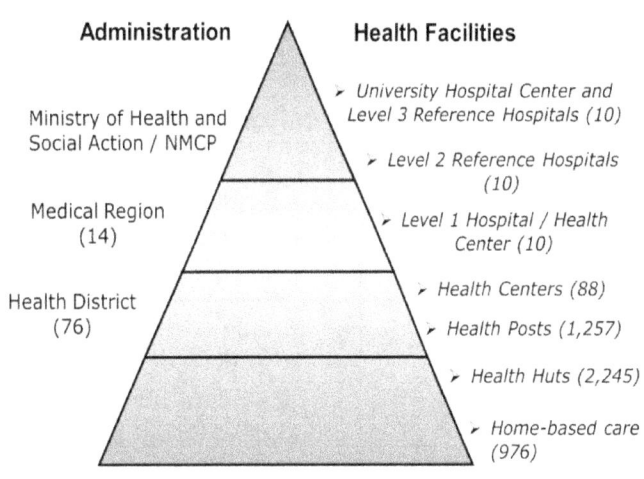

Senegal currently is divided into 76 health districts, each with at least one health center and a number of health posts that are staffed by chief nurses and sometimes midwives. There are approximately 1,257 health posts in Senegal. Although not a formal part of the health system, Senegal's health care pyramid rests on a foundation of approximately 2,245 "functional" health huts that are established and managed by local communities and cover approximately 50% of the country's population. A functional health hut is defined as one that has a trained community health worker (literacy is preferred but not required), regular supervision by the chief nurse of the health post, and the basic structure and equipment needed to provide services. The community health workers offer an integrated package of preventive and curative services or referral for more advanced medical care. Additional community health staff includes *matrones*, who are trained birth attendants; and *relais*, who are health educators and communicators. Since 2008, a new type of health worker, the village malaria worker (*dispensateur de soins à domicile (DSDOM)*), provides testing with RDTs and treatment with ACTs through the home-based management of malaria program (*prise en charge à domicile (PECADOM)*), now active in approximately 1,000 villages where health services are difficult to access. The DSDOMs work independently from their homes, without a formal health structure or management committee. A pilot project is now training DSDOMs in management of pneumonia and diarrhea in addition to malaria. Both health huts and DSDOMs are linked to their supervising health post by the commodity supply chain and the health information system (i.e. they get supplies from and submit data to the health post).

4. Country Malaria Control Strategy: Achieve Pre-Elimination by 2015

The NMCP's evaluation of the 2006-2010 National Strategic Plan for Malaria Control concluded that currently applicable interventions had been maximally scaled up given the resources available, with dramatic reductions in morbidity and mortality, but without interrupting transmission. In developing the 2011-2015 National Strategic Plan, the NMCP adopted a goal of reaching the threshold for pre-elimination (less than one case per 1,000 population) by 2015, continuing the use of proven interventions already scaled up nationally, adopting new proven interventions in a targeted manner, and piloting new interventions. Focus will be placed on zones with high population and endemicity. The plan also establishes the target of reducing malaria mortality by 75% from a 2010 baseline, using the following strategies and objectives:

Table 1: Objectives for the 2011-2015 National Strategic Plan for Malaria Control

Strategies	Objectives
Integrated vector management	• ≥ 80% of people sleep under an LLIN • ≥ 90% of people in targeted zones protected by IRS • ≥ 95% of productive larval sources treated in targeted zones
Malaria in pregnancy	• ≥80% of pregnant women receive two doses of IPTp • 100% of pregnant women with malaria treated with recommended antimalarials
Case management	• ≥ 95% of suspected cases of malaria tested with an RDT • Treat 100% of confirmed cases of malaria according to national policy
Epidemic preparedness	• Detect 80% of epidemics in a timely fashion • Bring every epidemic under control within two weeks of its detection
Management of procurement and stocks	• Ensure that ≥95% of health structures have RDTs and ACTs in stock

Communication for health promotion	• Reinforce health promotion in order to improve use of malaria control interventions
Monitoring and evaluation	• Insure prompt and complete reporting and use of data for monitoring and evaluation of the 2011-2015 National Strategic Plan
Program management	• Improve the management of the program at all levels

The 2011-2015 National Strategic Plan for Malaria Control outlines an integrated package of activities, which includes major efforts in integrated vector management, malaria in pregnancy, case management, epidemic prevention and control, pharmaceutical supply chain management, health promotion, program management, and monitoring and evaluation. Supporting interventions include human resource management, management and mobilization of financial resources, supply chain management, coordination of partnerships, and community mobilization. While the plan was written based on currently scaled up interventions, the NMCP is moving rapidly to adopt additional interventions (such as seasonal malaria chemoprevention (SMC) and pre-referral treatment) that are expected to help the program to reach its goals.

5. Integration, Collaboration and Coordination

Funding and Technical Partnerships
Senegal currently has one active **Global Fund** malaria grant, Round 10, an $88 million grant for 2012 to 2016, awarded to two principal recipients, the NMCP and IntraHealth International. Signing of the Round 10 grant was delayed by a year, and disbursement was then delayed by another 10 months. While some activities planned for that time period were cancelled, resulting in loss of funds, the NMCP is trying to implement all the activities for Phase 1 in a compressed timeframe to avoid losing additional funds or possibly compromising Phase 2.

The **World Bank** continues to provide support for malaria through the Senegal River Basin Development Organization and the Nutrition Enhancement Project. Activities include LLIN distribution and communication/education.

The World Health Organization (WHO) continues to provide technical and some financial support for the implementation of treatment and prevention policies, planning, M&E, research, surveillance, and management of the NMCP.

The United Nations Children's Fund (UNICEF) provides support for district-level health plans in the regions of Kolda, Sédhiou, Kédougou, Tambacounda and Matam. UNICEF collaborates with the United States Agency for International Development (USAID) funded Community Health Program Component to support various community health interventions in more than 500 health huts.

The Islamic Development Bank has provided $8 million in loans for the procurement of LLINs and RDTs, health personnel training, and support for supervision. One million LLINs and RDTs were procured through UNICEF with this funding with 600,000 of these LLINs used to carry out the first phase of UC activities in four regions in 2010.

11

In addition to multilateral institutions, Senegal benefits from the support of various bilateral donors. **The French Cooperation** contributes significantly to research activities through the *Institut Pasteur* and the *Institut de Recherche pour le Développement* (IRD) and places a technical advisor at the MOH. **The Japan International Cooperation Agency** (JICA) and USAID have developed a joint partnership in Tambacounda and Kedougou regions; JICA donated $1 million for malaria activities in these regions through UNICEF in 2013. **The Chinese Cooperation** makes an annual donation of drugs for the treatment of uncomplicated and severe malaria, and **the Embassy of Thailand** has supported the participation of health personnel at malaria training courses in Thailand. **The Belgian Technical Cooperation** is supporting the overall development of the health sector primarily in Fatick and Kaolack regions.

Senegal's non-governmental and faith-based partners are also numerous. **Medicos del Mundo** and several Spanish non-governmental organizations are active in Sédhiou and Kolda regions. They have supported outreach activities by health post staff, rehabilitation of health huts, and LLIN distribution campaign operations.

Malaria No More supported the dissemination of a variety of messages promoting malaria prevention and treatment through the "Senegal Surround Sound" campaign in collaboration with the **Youssou Ndour Foundation**. **Speak Up Africa** is a local non-governmental organization that grew out of these activities and is dedicated to mobilizing African leadership, resources and individual action against malaria, diarrhea, and pneumonia in several countries. In Senegal the group has supported various communications/advocacy activities and helps to draw in national celebrities to support the malaria control cause.

The **Senegalese Red Cross Society** has received funds from PMI via the International Federation of Red Cross and Red Crescent Societies, and contributed its own funds, to support volunteers and supervisors during the under-five and UC mass distribution campaigns and to implement follow-up activities encouraging net hanging and use. The **International Committee of the Red Cross** supports outreach activities and LLIN distribution campaign operations in conflict zones in Ziguinchor and Sédhiou regions.

The **Malaria Control and Evaluation Partnership for Africa** (MACEPA), which began work in Senegal in 2009, supported the development of the 2011-2015 National Strategic Plan and continues to support the NMCP through a pre-elimination project in one northern district, including enhanced and integrated surveillance and case investigation.

Senegal is fortunate to have strong academic and research capacities in epidemiology, parasitology and entomology at the NMCP, *Université Cheikh Anta Diop* (UCAD), the **Parasite Control Service,** IRD, and the *Institut Pasteur*. These groups have strong collaborative relationships and together have published much of the recent literature on malaria in Senegal.

Private Sector
In the private sector, the **Pfizer** pharmaceutical company implemented a malaria control program in three health districts in the Tambacounda Region from 2008 to 2011. The program focused on Behavior Change Communication (BCC) for improved care-seeking behavior, as well as

increasing access to care by making additional community health huts functional through staff training and provision of basic equipment.

In recent years the NMCP has been working with an increasing number of private enterprises on outreach and sensitization programs, LLIN distributions, and malaria case management, including **Total**(gas and oil), **BICIS** (bank), **Senegalese Sugar Company**, **Eiffage** (road construction), and **Bollore Africa Logistics**. **ADEMAS** is also working with the private sector through social marketing of LLINs in pharmacies and Total stations.

Within United States Government (USG)
The United States Peace Corps and PMI embarked on a new partnership in 2011. In Senegal, PMI staff and implementing partners continue to regularly participate in pre-service and in-service training sessions and over the past year supported one third-year malaria volunteer to further enhance collaboration on LLIN UC activities. Peace Corps volunteers also support PMI and the NMCP through information, education and communication (IEC) activities and participating in M&E and operational research (OR) activities.

Global Health Initiative
Malaria prevention and control is a major foreign assistance objective of the U.S. Government (USG). In May 2009, President Barack Obama announced the GHI, a six-year, comprehensive effort to reduce the burden of disease and promote healthy communities and families around the world. Through the GHI, the United States will help partner countries improve health outcomes, with a particular focus on improving the health of women, newborns and children. The GHI is a global commitment to invest in healthy and productive lives, building upon and expanding the USG's successes in addressing specific diseases and issues.

6. PMI Goals, Targets and Indicators

The goal of PMI is to reduce malaria-associated mortality by 70% compared to pre-initiative levels in the 15 original PMI countries by 2015. By the end of calendar year 2014, PMI will assist Senegal to achieve the following targets in populations at risk for malaria:
- >90% of households with a pregnant woman and/or children under five will own at least one ITN;
- 85% of children under five will have slept under an ITN the previous night;
- 85% of pregnant women will have slept under an ITN the previous night;
- 85% of houses in geographic areas targeted for IRS will have been sprayed;
- 85% of pregnant women and children under five will have slept under an ITN the previous night or in a house that has been sprayed with IRS in the last six months;
- 85% of women who have completed a pregnancy in the last two years will have received two or more doses of IPTp during that pregnancy; and
- 85% of government health facilities have ACTs available for treatment of uncomplicated malaria.

7. Progress on Coverage/Impact Indicators to Date

The table below shows that steady progress has been made for most malaria indicators in Senegal, as measured by two Demographic and Health Surveys (DHS) (2005 and 2010), two Malaria Indicator Surveys (MISs) (2006 and 2008), and the new continuous DHS. Of note, most of the surveys have taken place primarily during the dry season, when ITN use and parasitemia are generally lower, though this should not affect ITN ownership, IRS and IPTp coverage, or child mortality. The cDHS covered both rainy and dry seasons.

Household ownership of at least one ITN rose from 20% in 2005 to 82% in 2009 immediately after a mass distribution campaign targeting children under 5, but fell back to 63% in 2010. Three of the five regions in which UC campaigns had been conducted prior to the 2010 DHS had 94% household ITN ownership, but in Dakar, the most populous region, ownership was only 37%. The cDHS showed that ownership had risen to 73% in 2012-2013. Utilization of ITNs by children under five rose from 7% in 2006 to 46% in 2012. Similar trends in utilization were observed with pregnant women and in the general population.

The proportion of pregnant women receiving two doses of IPTp with sulfadoxine-pyrimethamine (SP) increased from 12% in 2005 to 52% in 2008, but fell to 39% in 2010 due primarily to stock outs of SP. A slight increase to 41% was noted in 2012. Comparing the proportion of children with fever who received prompt treatment with an ACT among the 2006, 2008, and 2010 surveys is difficult given the introduction of RDTs in late 2007, with treatment being given only to patients with a positive test. In addition, the diagnostic algorithm mandates that only those without an obvious alternate cause for fever be tested with an RDT. According to the 2010 DHS, 10% of children with fever in the last two weeks were reported to have received a diagnostic test, and 3% received an ACT within 24 hours of onset of fever.

As a result of the scale-up of malaria control interventions, parasitemia in children under five has fallen from 6% nationwide in 2008 to 3% nationwide in 2010, with this rate being maintained in 2012-13. The mortality rate for children under five has fallen from 121 deaths per 1,000 live births in the 2005 DHS to 65 in the 2012 cDHS.

Table 2: Evolution of Key Malaria Indicators in Senegal from 2005 to 2012

Indicator	2005 DHS[4]	2006 MIS[5]	2008 MIS[6]	2010 DHS[2]	cDHS Y1*
% Households with an ITN	20	36	60	63	73
% General population who slept under an ITN the previous night	6	12	23	29	41
% Children under five who slept under an ITN the previous night	7	16	29	35	46
% Pregnant women who slept under an ITN the previous night	9	17	29	37	43
Households in targeted districts protected by IRS	--	--	80	80	--
Households with an ITN or sprayed within previous 12 months	--	--	--	66	76
% Women who received two or more doses of IPTp during their last pregnancy in the last two years	12	49	52	39	41
% Children under five with fever in the last two weeks who received a diagnostic test	--	--	9	10	--
% Children under five with fever in the last two weeks who received treatment with an ACT within 24 hours of onset of fever	--	3	2	3	0.5
% Women of childbearing age with anemia (<11 g/dL)	59	--	64	54	--
% Children 6-59 months with severe anemia (<8 g/dL)	20	--	17	14	10
% Children under five with parasitemia (*P. falciparum*)	--	--	6	3	3
Under five mortality rate per 1,000 live births	121	--	85	72	65

*continuous DHS, Year 1, September 2012 – June 2013

8. Challenges, Opportunities, and Threats

Senegal has made great strides against malaria in the last decade, though challenges remain in virtually every domain of malaria prevention and treatment. Recent policy changes and innovative solutions being piloted provide opportunities to advance malaria control.

Challenges

Pharmaceutical Management: Management challenges at the Central Medical Stores (CMS), including delays in procuring and distributing essential medications, inadequate quantification, and poor responsiveness to program needs, represent a significant threat to successful program implementation. A new CMS director was appointed in August 2012 and is working to improve the system in collaboration with implementing partners. Poor supply chain management affects the availability of RDTs and ACTs at all levels, from hospitals to community health huts. There was a nationwide shortage of RDTs and ACTs in late 2012, as well as widespread ACT stock outs at the community level. During the data strike, data on RDT and ACT consumption were not reported, making quantification and resupply very difficult. In addition, there are concerns that district and health facility pharmacy managers neglect free commodities (such as ACTs, RDTs and SP) in favor of those that bring in revenue.

Data Availability: Historically, Senegal has had a very robust routine malaria information system; however, the data retention strike meant that the NMCP had no information on the number of suspected malaria cases, diagnostic tests performed, or confirmed cases. This compromised epidemic surveillance and planning for RDT and ACT procurement and prevented monitoring of program efficacy. Some health facilities did not even permit supervision visits during the data strike, limiting the ability of the NMCP to oversee malaria prevention and treatment activities. The data strike was formally lifted in March 2013, although it continues in some districts, and the process of rebuilding the routine health information system is underway. Active data collection from peripheral facilities to provide information on morbidity and mortality from 2010 through 2012 is nearly completed.

Insecticide Resistance: Insecticide resistance threatens both LLIN and IRS programs in Senegal, as it does in many PMI countries. Only three of the 15 surveillance sites showed sensitivity to pyrethroids in 2010 and none were in districts targeted for IRS. Carbamates are now being used in all IRS districts, although they have a shorter half-life than the pyrethroids used previously. One non-IRS district shows resistance to bendiocarb (a carbamate), and three districts show intermediate sensitivity, necessitating a change to organophosphates (which show complete sensitivity) and a decrease in the number of districts sprayed. While pyrethroid sensitivity has increased in districts sprayed with carbamates, given the strategy of UC with LLINs, a return to pyrethroids for IRS is not an option.

Donor Funding: The Senegal Global Fund Round 10 grant agreement was signed in December 2011, more than one year after the proposal was approved for funding, and the first disbursement was only made in October 2012. While some activities planned for that time period were cancelled, resulting in loss of funds, the NMCP is trying to implement all the activities for Phase 1 in a very compressed timeframe. Recently the Global Fund agreed to a nine-month no-cost extension to provide the NMCP more time to implement planned activities, and negotiations are underway for a costed extension through the end of 2014. During this time, Senegal will prepare its application for resources under the New Funding Model.

Opportunities
New Policies: Senegal has adopted a number of policy changes for case management, including treatment of pregnant women in their second and third trimesters with ACTs rather than quinine, pre-referral treatment of severe malaria with rectal artesunate, and implementation of SMC with sulfadoxine-pyrimethamine/amodiaquine (SP-AQ). Approximately half of malaria cases reported in Senegal occur in the four targeted regions, where access to prompt case management is difficult and morbidity and mortality remain high. SMC is being planned, documented and evaluated in order to maximize success and lessons learned in the implementation of this new

intervention at a large scale. Pre-referral rectal artesunate will be introduced nationwide in health posts, and at the community level as a pilot in one high transmission district prior to scale-up. A study in this region combining PECADOM, SMC, and pre-referral rectal artesunate decreased malaria incidence in children less than 10 years by 80% demonstrating the potential for dramatic reduction in malaria morbidity and mortality with scale-up of these interventions.[8]

Continuous Survey: Senegal is the first sub-Saharan African country to pilot a continuous survey, implementation of which began in October 2012, during the high transmission season. The continuous survey includes both population-based (DHS) and health facility (service provision assessment (SPA)) components. While balancing the needs of malaria and other programs is challenging, the continuous survey presents an opportunity to measure trends that will guide decision-making on a more frequent basis.

Collaboration with Peace Corps: The local partnership with Peace Corps was strengthened this year as a particularly motivated third year volunteer took the lead on coordinating the involvement of volunteers in field activities and channeling their ideas and questions to PMI and/or the NMCP. The more than 200 volunteers in-country represent a valuable resource for everything from testing communications materials to conducting household visits to gathering information on specific questions. In return, the PMI Resident Advisors provide technical assistance on specific volunteer projects, facilitate training sessions, and ensure that Peace Corps leadership has a place at the table when key malaria interventions are being planned and implemented.

Direct Funding: The USAID procurement reforms have given PMI/Senegal the opportunity to directly support its two strongest local partners – the NMCP and the University of Dakar. Previously, PMI channeled funds for these partners through WHO. Starting in FY 2012, PMI negotiated fixed amount reimbursement agreements with both entities to fund specific activities, including supervision, epidemic surveillance sites, and a malariology course (NMCP) as well as entomologic monitoring and drug efficacy testing (UCAD). The NMCP has proven itself to be very capable in managing large amounts of funding and complex programs, as evidenced by successful implementation of more than $80 million in Global Fund grants since 2005, and will receive an increasing proportion of PMI funds for implementation of specific activities, as capacity allows.

9. PMI Support Strategy

The support strategy for PMI in Senegal focuses on integration, complementarity and flexibility. A large proportion of PMI-supported activities are implemented through projects that also include other health domains (health system strengthening, community health, health service improvement, and health communication and promotion). This helps promote a rational use of USG resources, avoids having numerous vertical programs, and fosters synergy with other MOH entities. While some other technical and financial partners have strict geographic or programmatic restrictions on how their funds are used, PMI activities are implemented nationwide to the extent that this is indicated and we have been able to demonstrate great flexibility in reprogramming our funds in response to changing needs. This has occurred on numerous occasions, particularly related to blockages in disbursement of Global Fund resources.

PMI did not procure any ACTs or RDTs for its first three years of implementation, but was able to promptly pick up this critical element of the national strategy when problems arose in 2010. Finally, PMI supports and follows the country's strategy of testing new interventions on a relatively small scale and then expanding as soon as feasible based on the results of evaluations.

III.OPERATIONAL PLAN

1. Insecticide-Treated Nets

NMCP/PMI Objectives
The NMCP 2011-2015 Strategic Plan includes two key strategies for malaria prevention related to LLINs: 1) distribution of LLINs to achieve and maintain UC, defined as one treated net per sleeping space; and 2) reinforcement of behavior change communication on the use of LLINs. The objective is for 80% of the population to sleep under an LLIN every night by 2015. High coverage rates will be achieved and maintained through both mass and continuous distribution approaches.

Progress since PMI was launched
The NMCP and partners have supported various approaches for LLIN distribution: 1) periodic mass free distribution, 2) targeted subsidies for vulnerable groups, 3) untargeted subsidies through health facilities and community-based organizations (CBOs), and 4) commercial sales.

Periodic mass free distribution of LLINs: In 2007 the NMCP began to work with PMI and other partners on large-scale mass "catch-up" distributions of LLINs to children under five, culminating in a national campaign in 2009. Mass distributions targeting every sleeping space began in 2010 and were completed in early 2013, with more than 6.5 million LLINs distributed. The campaign started with high malaria transmission and/or underserved regions and progressively covered the country.

Targeted subsidies for vulnerable groups: From 2004 to 2009, PMI supported the subsidized sale of ITNs and later LLINs to pregnant women and children under five (360,000 nets distributed). This system involved agreements between facility health committees and private sector net distributors, with beneficiaries contributing a small copayment. Beginning in July 2012, free nets were made available to pregnant women during their first antenatal consultation.

Untargeted sales of subsidized bednets: From 2006 to 2007, the NMCP supported bednet sales to the general population at health facility pharmacies and through CBOs at a subsidized price of 1,000 West African Financial Community Francs (CFA) (about $2 per net), a portion of which was retained by the health districts and CBOs. Beginning in July 2012, PMI supported the introduction of a system to make subsidized nets available to clients frequenting health facilities at a price of 500 F CFA (about $1).

Commercial bednets sold at market prices to the general public: When PMI supported social marketing of LLINs until 2009, several major manufacturers supplied LLINs for sale in the private sector. Nearly 100,000 LLINs were sold between 2007 and 2009. With the advent of mass free distributions, however, the market for full-price nets was significantly weakened. ITNs can still be found in pharmacies and some shops, primarily in major urban areas, but they are generally not long-lasting varieties. These bednets are sold at 3,000 – 7,500 CFA ($7.15 – $17.90) each.

As a result of implementing these different strategies, household ownership of at least one ITN has increased substantially (from 20% in 2005 to 63% in 2010).Utilization of ITNs by children under five rose from 7% in 2006 to 35% in 2010, with similar trends observed among pregnant women and in the general population. However, these data mask significant disparities among regions. For example, Ziguinchor, Saint Louis and Fatick regions had not yet been reached by the universal coverage campaign at the time of the 2010 DHS but still had close to 80% possession and 50% utilization among children (except Fatick at 28%). Three of the five regions in which UC campaigns had been conducted prior to the 2010 DHS had 94% household ITN ownership, but in Dakar, the most populous region with persistent malaria hotspots, ownership was only 37% and use by children and pregnant women hovered around 15%.

Progress in the past 12 months
Senegal completed its national UC campaign in April 2013, with nearly three million LLINs distributed in Dakar and Thies Regions. This phase was supported almost entirely by the country's Global Fund Round 10 grants, although PMI staff and implementing partners continued to participate in the national coordinating committee and to provide technical assistance and local support. Beginning in July 2013, the NMCP also restarted mass distributions in the regions that were initially covered in 2010 (Kedougou, Tambacounda, Sedhiou, and Kolda). Approximately 92,000 LLINs were distributed in Kedougou, with the other regions planning their distributions before the end of the year. The Global Fund, JICA (via UNICEF) and Peace Corps/Against Malaria Foundation are all contributing nets and operational support.

With the goal of making LLINs widely available at reasonable cost, PMI shifted its focus this year to the different continuous distribution channels that have been adopted or are being tested. To date, approximately 342,000 LLINs have been distributed through the following channels, almost exclusively with PMI support

1) Health system: The program that started in July 2012 was expanded to the remaining two regions in March (these regions had been implementing their mass distribution campaigns at the time the others started). Free LLINs are given to pregnant women during their first antenatal care (ANC) visit and subsidized LLINs are sold for 500 F CFA (approximately $1) to all other clients utilizing health services. Between January and September 2013, approximately 95,000 LLINs were distributed to pregnant women and 128,000 were sold to other health facility clients (total 223,000 LLINs). IntraHealth International, under its Global Fund grant, supported some transportation costs.

2) Community: Subsidized distribution via community-based organizations began in Louga and Ziguinchor regions in March 2013. To date 105 community-based organizations (CBOs) in thirteen districts have been enrolled in the program. Community "relays" distribute coupons during home visits or from a fixed point and individuals then redeem the coupons at distribution sites. As with the health facility channel, the LLINs are sold

for 500 F CFA (approximately $1) and the copay is shared at different levels to cover transport costs and communications activities. More than 30,000 LLINs were distributed via this channel from March to September 2013.

3) Schools: PMI supported the free distribution of LLINs to students in classes CI and CE2 (six- and nine-year olds) once during the school year. The distributions were accompanied by educational activities. During the pilot, 75,710 LLINs were distributed via this channel in Louga and Ziguinchor regions. The CBO and school channels will be evaluated after a few months to determine what should be scaled-up and how.

4) Social marketing: The subsidized sale of LLINs began in pharmacies and gas station shops in August 2013. The nets are sold at a price of 1,000 F CFA (approximately $2) and are branded with a unique logo and promoted through a communications campaign that focuses on being a protective head of household. PMI provides the LLINs to pharmaceutical wholesalers, who then assure distribution through their normal supply chain. Actors at each level of the supply chain retain the profit from the sale of LLINs to cover their operational costs. To date, more than 13,000 LLINs have been distributed to private pharmacies for sale to consumers.

Opportunities:
Collaboration with local community development and education authorities has been very strong in the pilot regions. This has lessened the burden on the health actors and brought new perspectives to the program. The system has continued to function well even following the pilot period, with as many LLINs distributed in the four months after direct support ended as were distributed during the pilot.

Challenges:
The health system channel faced supply challenges in its first year for two reasons: 1) the data retention strike meant that most districts did not submit reports on their continuous distribution activities and were thus ineligible to have their stocks replenished; and 2) the CMS were not able to transport nets to the regions as had been envisioned. Thus, only those health districts near warehouses in Dakar and Thies and those who submitted reports had consistent LLIN stocks. The supply problem began to be resolved in January when Global Fund resources were mobilized to contract with a private company to transport nets and with the end of the data strike in March 2013.

Commodity gap analysis
Senegal completed its nationwide universal coverage mass distribution campaign in April 2013, and began covering the initial four regions (whose UC campaigns began in 2010) for a second time. Subsequently maintaining high coverage levels with LLINs will require keeping up and expanding the different routine channels across the country. Approximately two million nets need to be distributed through the routine channels every year in order to maintain coverage. The next mass distribution campaign is tentatively planned for 2015 and will cover the regions that had their first UC campaigns in 2011 and 2012. As multiple routine channels will be operational in those regions during 2014, people will have several options to be able to replace worn out nets in the interim.

Table 3: LLIN Gap Analysis

Calendar Year	2013	2014	2015
Total Population	**13,077,497**	**13,391,357**	**13,712,749**
Routine Distribution Needs[1]			
Pregnant women during first prenatal care visit (3.9% of the population); assumes 100% attendance for one visit	510,022	522,263	534,797
Other health facility clients; assumes 10% of all clients will request an ITN[2]	733,648	751,255	769,285
Community-based organizations	359,917	348,417	335,767
Primary school students	237,163	310,347	318,207
Social marketing	115,000	126,500	139,150
Estimated total need for routine channels	*1,955,750*	*2,058,782*	*2,097,206*
Mass Distribution Needs			
2013 campaign – Dakar, Thies, Kedougou, Kolda Tambacounda, Sedhiou	4,327,850		
2015 campaign – Kaffrine, Kaolack, Diourbel, Fatick, Saint Louis, Matam, Louga Ziguinchor			3,832,400
Estimated total need for mass campaigns	*4,327,850*	*0*	*3,832,400*
Total Routine and Mass ITN Needs	6,283,600	2,058,782	5,929,606
Partner Contributions			
PMI (primarily routine channels)	1,500,000	1,000,000	1,000,000
Global Fund (mass distribution)	3,615,346	2,653,427	2,379,049
Peace Corps / Against Malaria Foundation	680,000		
UNICEF/JICA	90,000		
Total Partner Contributions	**5,885,346**	**3,653,427**	**3,379,049**
Gap [3]	**398,254**	**(1,594,645)**	**2,550,557**

[1] Routine needs based primarily on 2012 continuous distribution assessment (NetCalc), with some updates

[2] Assumptions about proportion of clients requesting an ITN will be reviewed based on actual sales

[3] The 2013 gap is fictional as the needs for CBOs, schools and social marketing were calculated based on a full year of implementation nationwide. In reality, CBOs and school channels are only operational in two regions to date, with scale-up planned for the last quarter of 2013. Social marketing is starting at the end of July 2013.

PMI plans to provide approximately one million of the needed LLINs each year, which will be distributed primarily through the routine channels. If Senegal successfully passes to the second phase of funding under its Global Fund Round 10 grant, more than two million LLINs are expected to be procured through that mechanism. The apparent surplus of LLINs in 2014 will be used to cover the gap in 2015.

Plans and justification
With FY 2014 funds, PMI and the NMCP plan to focus efforts on maintaining a constant supply of nets and a strong, nationwide routine distribution system for ITNs as described above, while potentially restarting mass distributions. PMI also plans to support communications activities to inform the population about how to acquire nets and their proper use and maintenance. These activities are described in the BCC section.

Description and budget for proposed activities: ($4,800,000)

1. *Procurement ($4,000,000) and operational support ($800,000) for distribution of LLINs*
PMI plans to primarily support the routine LLIN distribution channels by procuring approximately one million LLINs and supporting operational costs. Operational costs are expected to decrease once the continuous channels are fully functional nationwide, but will continue to include transportation to regions/districts and supervision. Nets may be provided to fill gaps for mass distribution activities if needed.

2. Indoor Residual Spraying

NMCP/PMI Objectives
Senegal's 2011-2015 Strategic Plan includes IRS as a key strategy for malaria prevention in Senegal along with other vector control interventions, such as LLINs and larval source management. The goal for IRS is to protect at least 90% of the population in targeted districts by 2015.

Progress since PMI was launched
Senegal has benefitted from IRS since PMI began work in the country in 2007. The first three districts sprayed with PMI support- Richard Toll, Nioro and Velingara - each represented different ecological zones. One spray round was carried out just before the high transmission season in each district, while in Richard Toll, a district along the Senegal River, an additional round was done immediately prior to the second seasonal peak in April. After entomological monitoring demonstrated that the insecticidal activity persisted long enough to cover the second peak, this second round was eliminated in 2010. Also in 2010, IRS operations were expanded to Guinguineo, Malem Hodar and Koumpentouom, districts that were among the 16 health districts prioritized for IRS by the NMCP. In 2011, because malaria rates were low and insecticide resistance was high in Richard Toll, spray operations ceased in this district and Koungheul was selected as a replacement.

The population protected during the six years of IRS ranged from around 650,000 to more than 1 million in 2012 with high coverage rates being achieved in most years (see Table 4).

Table 4: IRS Coverage

Year (no. districts)	2007 (3)	2008 (3)	2009 (3)	2010 (6)	2011 (5)	2012 (6)
Structures targeted	*	162,439	200,761	259,967	244,855	312,938
Structures sprayed	*	153,942	176,279	254,559	240,770	306,916
Coverage rate	*	95%	88%	98%	98%	98%
Population protected	678,971	645,346	661,814	959,727	887,315	1,095,093

* In 2007 data were collected on number of households, not number of structures

Pyrethroids were used during the first four years of spray operations, but a significant drop in insecticide susceptibility of mosquitoes to pyrethroids was observed and the decision was made to switch to a carbamate for the 2011 operations. Insecticide susceptibility to pyrethroids increased after this rotation to a carbamate.

Spray operations have been organized by PMI implementing partners under the direction of the NMCP, the Hygiene Service, UCAD, and district health management teams. PMI support includes training and equipping locally-recruited spraying agents with help from the NMCP and its vector-control partners, with supervision by the Hygiene Service. All spray rounds were followed by post-spray evaluation meetings to identify lessons learned and opportunities for improving the next round. As a result, the NMCP is now well-prepared to assume more responsibility for IRS operations.

Progress in the last 12 months

Entomologic Monitoring: During the eight months following the end of the 2012 spray round, entomologists from UCAD, the Parasite Control Service, *Institut Pasteur*, and IRD conducted entomologic monitoring in five villages in each of the six IRS districts and three villages in two neighboring untreated districts, Kolda and Kaffrine. The monitoring included cone bioassays on walls to test for insecticidal activity (not in the non-IRS districts), knockdown spray catches and human landing catches. Because susceptibility to carbamate was still high at the end of the 2011 spray round, this class of insecticide was selected for the 2012 spray season. Results of cone bioassays on bendiocarb-sprayed walls were highly variable and were district-dependent, suggesting that the quality of spray operations had been better in some districts than others. Within one month of spraying, the mean mosquito mortality per district ranged from 71% (Velingara) to 99% (Malem Hodar). By the second month after spraying, the mean mosquito mortality observed was as high as 84% (Malem Hodar) but was as low as 42% (Guinguineo). By the third month after spraying the mortality was low in all districts, even in Malem Hodar, where it was 40%. Thus, the insecticidal activity of bendiocarb appeared to endure at most two months. In a few districts, cone bioassays were also done with mosquitoes raised from locally collected larvae. Mortality rates on the walls were even lower, although the mosquitos were 96% to 100% susceptible to bendiocarb in resistance assays. Interestingly, as was observed in 2011, an apparent increase of insecticidal activity was noted in cone bioassays in all the districts in the sixth to eighth months after spraying, a phenomenon that will be investigated further to determine whether other factors are playing a role in the mortality of the test mosquitoes. Parity rates of mosquitoes collected in the IRS districts of Malem Hodar and Velingara were lower than those collected in the neighboring non-IRS districts of Kaffrine and Kolda, suggesting that insecticide was still reducing vector longevity.

The insecticide resistance assays of 2012 showed that vector susceptibility to bendiocarb remained high, 98%-100% in the populations tested. In addition, the 2012 assays confirmed the return to higher levels of pyrethroid susceptibility observed in mosquitos of districts where bendiocarb had been used in 2011. For example, in Velingara the percentage of mosquitoes susceptible to deltamethrin increased from 58% in 2010 to 97% in 2011 and remained at 95% in 2012 and to permethrin from 50% to 94% and 91%. These data support a strategy of using alternate insecticide classes to restore vector sensitivity to pyrethroids and thus prolong the usefulness of LLINs, however it is not clear whether the increased sensitivity will continue or if this would permit a return to pyrethroids for IRS.

Spray Operations: In early 2013, the IRS Steering Committee, composed of representatives from NMCP, entomologists from UCAD, the National Hygiene Service, the National Directorate of Environment and Agriculture, the IRS implementing partner, and PMI made the decision to cease IRS operations in the districts of Guinguinéo and Nioro. Data indicated that malaria rates had become so low that IRS in these districts was no longer cost-effective. A plan for post-withdrawal action was prepared, including communications at both administrative and community levels and enhanced surveillance. Preparations for operations in the other four districts began in February, including reviewing training tools, selecting offices, preparing pits, recruiting seasonal spray operators, and training them. A census of eligible structures was also introduced to aid in the estimation of insecticide needs and to avoid insecticide stock outs experienced during the previous spray season. Actual spraying activities began in July, later than in previous years in order to ensure optimal coverage of the transmission season given the short duration of bendiocarb action. Because little resistance to bendiocarb was detected after the 2012 spray round, it was used again in 2013. All four districts (Koungheul, Koumpentoum, Malem Hodar, and Velingara) benefited from previous spray rounds. A total of 206,704 structures were sprayed (98% of those visited and eligible for spraying) and 690,090 people were protected. Despite the many challenges involved in IRS implementation, routine monitoring of spray operations suggests that high rates of acceptance have been consistently achieved in all spray rounds.

Opportunities
With each spray round, PMI places increasing emphasis on building national and local capacity for IRS. To date, agents of the National Hygiene Service and MOH personnel at many levels of the health system have been engaged in IRS activities. During the 2013 spray round, the NMCP assumed responsibility for implementing IEC operations in all districts. In 2014, the NMCP will assume responsibility for implementation of all IRS activities, with the exception of procurement, for one district. The national IRS Steering Committee will be intimately involved in this transition.

Plans and Justification
With FY 2014 funds, PMI plans to support spray operations and entomological monitoring in four districts. Dependent upon the successful implementation in the pilot district during the 2014

spray season, the NMCP will assume the majority of the operational responsibilities (except commodity procurement), including planning, IEC, training, and implementation of IRS activities with some technical assistance provided by PMI's implementing partner. Prior to the handover, PMI will take all necessary steps to ensure that the NMCP is ready to assume these technical and financial responsibilities, and will closely monitor implementation. The insecticide chosen for FY2014 will be a long-acting organophosphate.

Proposed activities with FY 2014 funding ($5,232,000)

1. *IRS Operations ($4,800,000)*
With FY 2014 funds, PMI plans to support one round of spray operations in four districts covering a population of approximately 740,000 people and 215,000 structures. With the challenges of insecticide resistance and rising costs, PMI does not plan to expand its support for IRS beyond four districts.

2. *Entomologic monitoring ($432,000)*
PMI plans to continue to support entomologists from UCAD and *Institut Pasteur* to conduct entomologic M&E for IRS as well as insecticide resistance monitoring. Entomologists will conduct cone bioassays immediately after spraying and at monthly intervals in all four spray districts. Vector behavior, will be assessed by monitoring indoor and outdoor biting rates and indoor resting densities. Parity rates will aid in determining female longevity and transmission potential. Finally, mosquito strains will be identified and checked for malaria sporozoites. Entomologists will continue to conduct insecticide susceptibility assays in the four spray districts, the districts where IRS operations have ceased, as well as in additional sites throughout the country where entomologists have been following the evolution of insecticide resistance during the past several years. An entomologist from Centers for Disease Control and Prevention (CDC) will provide TA for the planning and implementation of all PMI-funded entomologic monitoring activities as well as some supplies that have been difficult to obtain through other channels.

3. **Malaria in Pregnancy**

Malaria in Pregnancy

NMCP/PMI Objectives
Intermittent preventive therapy in pregnant women with SP given free-of-charge as directly observed therapy during focused ANC visits was adopted as national policy by the NMCP in 2003 and is implemented in all ANC sites nationwide. The NMCP objective is for 85% of women who have completed a pregnancy in the last two years to have received two or more doses of IPTp during that pregnancy. In addition, the NMCP aims to treat 100% of pregnant women with confirmed malaria according to national guidelines. The NMCP's strategy for increasing IPTp uptake includes advocacy for health workers and the population at large, training and supportive supervision of health workers, and outreach activities by health post staff to provide ANC services at the community level, all of which are supported by PMI.

Progress since PMI was launched

ANC attendance is high; 93% of pregnant women have at least one visit, but coverage of two doses of IPTp remains under 50%.[3] PMI has supported the production, dissemination, and use by health care workers of new ANC registers and ANC cards that allow for accurate recording of IPTp treatments; job aids to promote the correct management of malaria in pregnancy and improve the counseling skills of health care providers; water filters/dispensers and re-usable cups for SP administration; and refresher training and supportive supervision. The PMI-supported MIP training is part of an integrated ANC training and covers data collection and record-keeping, the prevention of MIP including IPTp with SP and use of LLINs, and diagnosis and case management of malaria in pregnancy with quinine. PMI also supports a routine LLIN distribution system that offers free LLINs to women attending ANC.

Progress during the last 12 months
Since October 2012, 278 facility-based health workers have been trained in the prevention, diagnosis, and treatment of malaria, including MIP. More than 1,500 outreach visits were made to health huts, resulting in 16,130 prenatal consultations and 9,677 doses of IPTp distributed.

Following the WHO recommendation, the NMCP has changed its case management policy to allow the treatment of pregnant women diagnosed with uncomplicated malaria during the second and third trimesters with ACTs, and has updated the policy, guidelines, and training manuals to incorporate WHO recommendations for simplification of IPTp guidelines. Quinine continues to be used to treat uncomplicated malaria in pregnant women during the first trimester, and in cases showing signs of severity.

Commodity Gap Analysis
SP for an anticipated 528,000 pregnant women is expected to be procured by the CMS. Fewer than 7,000 cases of malaria are reported among pregnant women annually; the ACTs needed to treat them are included in the overall ACT gap analysis in the case management section. The CMS also procures quinine for use in severe malaria cases and maintains adequate stocks.

Plans and Justification
PMI plans to continue to support activities aimed at reinforcing the provision of effective MIP services in health facilities in all regions in Senegal. Support is planned to continue for monitoring and supportive supervision of MIP service delivery, improvement of data collection including IPTp data, and training of new staff on IPTp, the importance of LLIN use in pregnancy, diagnosis and management of MIP, and counseling and interpersonal communication skills. PMI plans to continue to encourage collaboration between the NMCP and the Division of Reproductive Health to strengthen and streamline MIP activities.

Proposed activities with FY 2014 funding ($600,000)

1. *Reinforce provision of effective malaria in pregnancy services in health facilities and through outreach strategies*
PMI plans to update, print, and disseminate training materials and job aids to reflect new treatment recommendations and simplification of IPTp administration guidelines, and train health facility level providers on prevention and treatment of malaria during pregnancy. PMI also plans to continue to provide cups and water filters as needed for directly-observed treatment with

SP. Support for ANC outreach activities at health huts are planned to continue. Activities covered in other sections include the provision of free LLINs during the first ANC visit and BCC to reinforce ANC attendance, the importance of IPTp and the need to sleep under an LLIN each night.

4. Case Management

NMCP/PMI Objectives
PMI's objectives are:
- 85% of government health facilities have ACTs available for treatment of uncomplicated malaria
- 85% of children under five with suspected malaria will have received treatment with ACTs within 24 hours of onset of their symptoms

The NMCP's objectives also include:
- 95% of suspected malaria cases tested with an RDT
- 100% of confirmed cases treated according to national guidelines

The NMCP has adopted WHO recommendations regarding case investigation in districts in which annual incidence is less than 1/1000 and active case detection in hotspots in districts in which annual incidence is less than 15/1000. Given the goal of achieving pre-elimination nationally (incidence of symptomatic malaria less than 5/1000) in 2015, the need for RDTs for active case detection, as well as treatment for asymptomatic cases detected by these investigations, has increased.

Progress since PMI was launched
The NMCP adopted ACTs as first-line treatment in 2006 and introduced RDTs in 2007. Both AL and AS-AQ were adopted simultaneously as first-line drugs, with AS-AQ being procured from the beginning, and AL procured starting in 2010. While dihydroartemisinin-piperaquine was not formally adopted as a first-line therapy, annual donations of this product from the Chinese government are also used in the public health sector. Quinine is used for treatment of severe malaria in all age groups and in pregnant women in the first trimester.

Rapid diagnostic tests were introduced in formal health facilities in late 2007, along with a diagnostic algorithm specifying that if another obvious cause of fever was present, a patient would not be tested with an RDT nor be reported as a suspected malaria case, but be treated for that illness and be eligible to return for re-evaluation, including an RDT, if symptoms persisted. At the community level, RDTs were introduced in 2008, and all fevers are eligible for testing. Positive cases showing no signs of complications are treated with ACTs, while negative cases are referred to the nearest health post.

Two WHO recommendations recently adopted as policy are: (1) pre-referral treatment with rectal artesunate for severe malaria, to be introduced first at the health post level and subsequently at the community level (health huts and PECADOM); and (2) SMC with one treatment of SP-AQ monthly during the rainy season. Much of the research on SMC was conducted in Senegal, first in children under five, and subsequently in children up to ten years of age, including a multi-district trial involving 175,000 children (Badara Cisse, in press). Other research conducted in Senegal has had excellent results introducing both SMC and pre-referral treatment with rectal artesunate at the community level (Tine 2011).In Senegal, four southern regions (Sedhiou, Kolda, Tambacounda and Kedougou) are judged to meet all the WHO criteria for SMC (at least 60% of cases within four months, at least 10% annual incidence among children). In these regions, the months of August through November account for an average of 64% of annual cases. Implementation of SMC is planned to be through a door-to-door campaign over four months in the highest transmission region (Kedougou), and over three months in the remaining three regions. This is expected to adequately cover the peak transmission season.

PMI has supported both diagnostics and treatment of malaria through integrated training of health care providers at all levels, supportive supervision, and commodity procurement. In addition, PMI has provided microscopes, trained laboratory technicians, and supported quality assurance/quality control systems for microscopy.

Progress during the last 12 months
Diagnosis: PMI procured 300,000 RDTs for use in the formal health sector and at the community level. PMI supported the training of 88 laboratory technicians on malaria microscopy and supervision/quality control visits to 25 facility laboratories to date. During the quality control visits, the supervisors verify five negative and five positive slides that the microscopists have read, then have the microscopists read a panel of pre-selected slides. In addition, 10 positive and 10 negative slides are sent to Dakar for concurrence by the UCAD reference lab. A CDC diagnostics subject matter expert reviewed the microscopic training, supervision, and quality control program and provided recommendations to strengthen it.

Data collection began this year for a PMI-funded operations research project that seeks to determine the proportion of patients not tested with an RDT according to the NMCP's diagnostic algorithm who actually have parasitemia. (See M&E section for more details.)

The NMCP, with support from Malaria Control and Evaluation Partnership for Africa, piloted a case investigation strategy in the low-transmission district of Richard Toll. All household members of an index malaria case, as well as the members of the five surrounding households, were tested with RDTs. In over 140 cases investigated, 30 additional malaria cases were identified, most of them in the household of the index case. The NMCP plans to expand the pilot, screening only members of the immediate household, in adjacent low-transmission districts.

Treatment: PMI procured 345,000 ACT treatments, covering approximately half of the country's needs for the year. Case management activities in the formal health sector included training and supportive supervision, using a strategy of peer supervision and mentoring termed *TutoratPlus* in some districts. PMI supported the training of 277 health workers at the facility level and 800 at the community level on malaria case management including RDTs and ACTs. At the community level, both health huts offering an integrated package of activities including malaria case management with RDTs and ACTs and the home-based PECADOM program are included. The community-level program now includes a total of 2,143 health huts and 1,647 sites (all those that are functional in the country), as well as 976 DSDOMs. Since2012, PMI has supported integrated case management of pneumonia, diarrhea, and malaria in the PECADOM program, with 517 DSDOMs trained to date.

Implementation of SMC began in November 2013 in four south-eastern districts. PMI procured the drugs and worked closely with the NMCP to develop the implementation and monitoring plan. UNICEF supported operational costs for this phase, using resources allocated by Japan International Cooperation Agency for malaria programming. The strategy is based on three doses of SP-AQ for children 3-120 months, one dose monthly for two months (Due to the delay in receiving drugs, the campaign was implemented at the end of the high transmission season.). Approximately 53,000 children were treated. This new intervention is being rigorously monitored and evaluated using routine morbidity and mortality data, a case-control study, and process indicators.

Finally, to support the introduction of pre-referral treatment for severe malaria with rectal artesunate, national guidelines and manuals were updated. PMI procured 32,000 artesunate suppositories to treat an estimated 13,000 patients. Training for health providers is expected to take place in 2014.

Commodity Gap Analysis
The table below presents the gap analysis for ACTs and RDTs that the NMCP prepared during a quantification meeting with stakeholders. Due to the data retention strike, data on morbidity and incidence trends are not available for recent years. The estimates are based on quantities ordered by health districts and deliveries from the central and regional medical stores. From 2008 to 2012, ACT orders declined by approximately 5% per year. For RDTs, an increase of approximately 13% per year was observed. These rates were applied for out years, and a three-month buffer stock was added, to arrive at the commodity requirements presented below.

Table 5: ACT and RDT Gap Analysis

ACTs	2013	2014	2015	2016
ACT needs	844,312	799,460	756,991	716,778
Partner contributions	828,446*	700,000	600,000	0
Gap (Surplus)	15,866	99,460	156,991	716,778
RDTs	**2013**	**2014**	**2015**	**2016**
RDT needs	1,732,710	1,936,882	2,225,896	2,522,867
Partner contributions	1,854,400*	2,000,000	2,225,896	0
Gap (Surplus)	(121,690)	(63,118)	0	2,522,867

Stock currently in-country plus expected deliveries

Plans and Justification
PMI plans to support training and supervision for microscopic diagnosis of malaria, quality control for microscopy, and procurement of laboratory consumables and RDTs. The number of RDTs required is expected to increase as more case investigation and active case detection activities are carried out in the context of pre-elimination. PMI also plans to support training and supportive supervision to maintain quality of case management with RDTs and ACTs both in the formal health sector and at the community level (both health huts and home-based management).

PMI plans to continue its support for SMC in the high transmission regions of Senegal. Finally, PMI plans to continue to support pre-referral treatment for severe malaria, introduced in 2013, in an effort to significantly reduce malaria mortality. No other partners are expected to provide RDTs or ACTs during this period.

Proposed activities with FY 2014 funding ($5,026,000)

Diagnosis
1. *Strengthening microscopic diagnosis of malaria ($200,000)*
PMI plans to continue to provide training in microscopic diagnosis of malaria for new microscopists, as well as refresher training for those needing it. PMI plans to provide supportive supervision of malaria diagnosis by microscopy for laboratory and health facility staff and assist the NMCP and its partners to implement the quality assurance and control standards for malaria diagnostic testing. Sites showing poor performance will be targeted for additional on-site training and quality control visits.

2. *Microscopes and laboratory consumables ($50,000)*
PMI plans to provide microscopes and laboratory consumables to new health district laboratories, and to replace aging microscopes if needed.

3. *Procurement of RDTs ($1,396,000)*
The NMCP has requested that PMI procure approximately 2.2 million RDTs to cover nationwide needs, including diagnosis of symptomatic patients at health facilities, case investigation, and active case detection where indicated.

Treatment
1. *Improve case management at health facilities ($550,000)*
As part of the effort to improve the management of uncomplicated malaria with ACTs, PMI plans to support training for health care workers in case management with RDTs and ACTs (initial and refresher training, as indicated). Implementing partners will work with the MOH to provide supportive supervision in the correct management of malaria at health posts, health centers and hospitals.

2. *Strengthen community case management ($500,000)*
With FY2014 funding, PMI plans to continue to provide technical support on correct diagnosis, treatment, stock management, and referral practices for CHWs at health huts, and on timely data collection and integration of community case management data into the MOH reporting system. The PMI funding will complement other USAID/MCH funding to support the training, supervision, and monitoring of community-based staff.

3. *Support for home-based management of malaria (PECADOM) ($450,000)*
PMI plans to continue to support training and supervision of village malaria workers in malaria diagnosis with RDTs and treatment with ACTs as part of an integrated case management package that includes case management of acute respiratory infections and diarrhea. PMI plans to also support health post nurses in their supervision of DSDOMs. This activity is co-funded by USAID maternal-child health funds/partners.

4. *Procure ACTs ($525,000)*

PMI plans to procure approximately 600,000 ACT treatments, which will meet the majority of the country's needs for the year. Artemether-lumefantrine is planned to be procured and distribution targeted to the four regions in which SMC is implemented to avoid treating confirmed malaria cases with the same drug that is used for chemoprevention (amodiaquine). In previous years, approximately half of the country's malaria cases have occurred in these regions. Artesunate-amodiaquine is planned to be procured and targeted to the remaining regions.

5. *Operational costs ($900,000) and procurement of drugs ($542,000) for implementation of SMC*

PMI plans to continue to fund SMC with three doses of SP-AQ for children from six months to ten years to the four highest transmission regions. The age groups and geographic zones may be re-evaluated based on the initial experience in 2013. The operational funds are slated to support training, job aids, M&E, and supervision. The intervention should cover approximately 600,000 children for three months, with Kedougou region adding a fourth month to cover a longer transmission season. UNICEF is supporting operational costs during the first year of the campaign, but it is not yet known whether that support will continue or if other partners will join the effort. PMI plans to support the NMCP to get maximum participation and support from other malaria partners.

6. *Procurement of rectal artesunate suppositories ($25,000)*

PMI plans to continue to procure rectal artesunate for pre-referral treatment for severe malaria, currently estimated at approximately 13,000 treatments. The budget/quantity may be revised upwards if the community-level intervention being tested in 2013 proves successful.

7. *Therapeutic efficacy monitoring ($100,000)*

PMI plans to support therapeutic efficacy studies at two sites to monitor the susceptibility of *P. falciparum* to the first-line ACTs (artesunate-amodiaquine and artemether-lumefantrine) and monitoring of resistance markers for SP and amodiaquine in areas of SMC implementation.

5. Monitoring and Evaluation/Operations Research

NMCP/PMI Objectives

The NMCP objective for M&E is to ensure prompt and complete reporting and use of data for M&E of the 2011-2015 National Strategic Plan. The approach also includes surveillance and operational research targeted to reaching pre-elimination in 2015.

Progress since PMI was launched

Senegal was known for its robust routine malaria information system during the first few years of PMI implementation, providing data to guide and measure scale-up of malaria control activities. In this system, all relevant malaria data flowed up from the community-level (health huts and DSDOM) through health posts and districts, which then sent them to regional and central levels. The NMCP maintains a database of morbidity data by health post. The NMCP organized quarterly review meetings with health districts to share morbidity and mortality data as well as policy/technical information. This system was adversely impacted by a nationwide data retention strike in public health facilities from June 2010-March 2013. The quarterly review meetings resumed in July 2013.

Multiple national-level household surveys have been conducted to provide information on key malaria indicators, including MISs in 2006 and 2008, and DHSs in 2005 and 2010, and a post-campaign survey in 2009 to assess the ownership and use of ITNs after a campaign targeting children under five years of age. Senegal is now implementing a Continuous Survey consisting of population-based (DHS) and service provision assessment components, which will provide information to guide programming on a more regular basis (see details below).

A system of epidemic surveillance sites has been operational since 2008, starting in the Senegal River Valley. Ten districts are now enrolled in the program, with two sites each reporting morbidity, mortality and stock information on a weekly basis. Entomological monitoring of IRS districts and select non-IRS sites has guided IRS implementation, and PMI continues to support therapeutic efficacy testing and drug quality monitoring. Table 6 below summarizes the different M&E activities that have been supported by PMI as well as other partners.

Progress in the last 12 months

PMI provided TA to the NMCP for the development of guidelines for M&E, and for malaria surveillance, as well as support for a pilot project to collect data using tablet computers during supervision visits to facilitate analysis, which will be scaled up if successful. The majority of the epidemic surveillance sites continued to send weekly data to the NMCP during the data strike, serving as the NMCP's only window to malaria related morbidity/mortality. For the past several years the NMCP has disseminated the weekly spreadsheets to a large and varied group of stakeholders, and this year, the program developed a surveillance bulletin that presents the data in a more user-friendly format and includes analysis of different trends. The data strike affecting routine data was lifted in March, and the process of backfilling the databases and rebuilding the health information system is nearly complete.

Table 6: Monitoring and Evaluation Activities

Data Source	Activities	Year (2006-2014)								
		'06	'07	'08	'09	'10	'11	'12	'13	'14
Household Surveys	Demographic and Health Survey*					X				
	Continuous Demographic and Health Survey							X	X	X
	Malaria Indicator Survey*	X		X						
	Nationwide post-LLIN distribution campaign survey*				X					
	Universal coverage evaluation*						X			
Entomological monitoring	Entomologic monitoring*		X	X	X	X	X	X	X	X
Malaria Surveillance and Routine System support	Malaria epidemic surveillance*		X	X	X	X	X	X	X	X
	Impact Evaluation								X	
	Evaluation of NMCP strategic plan					X				
	M&E course					X	X	X	X	X
	Demographic Surveillance System		X	X						
	Therapeutic efficacy testing		X	X		X		X	X	X
	Drug quality monitoring*		X	X	X	X	X	X	X	X

*data available

The Continuous Survey, consisting of population-based (DHS) and health facility service provision assessment (SPA) components, completed one year of data collection. Two hundred clusters for the DHS, and a random sample of approximately 20% of health facilities for the SPA, were included. The Continuous Survey will provide annual estimates of all standard household-level malaria indicators (including anemia and parasitemia) as well as information on the available and quality of services in the health sector (including private providers).Results will be available nationally and by urban/rural and epidemiologic strata annually, and by region every two years. Preliminary results from the first round of data collection were disseminated in September 2013. This activity is supported by USAID, using malaria and other funds, as well as other partners including the MOH, the World Bank and UNICEF.

PMI provided TA to the NMCP for analysis of data collected during program implementation and preparation of abstracts to be presented at the American Society for Tropical Medicine and Hygiene annual conference. Five abstracts were accepted for presentation.

The Impact Evaluation process started with the formation of a steering committee by the Minister of Health, the recruitment of a local consultant, and validation of the work plan. The senior consultant is working with two other experts who have strong backgrounds in epidemiology and public health. The steering committee is composed of members with diverse expertise who are engaged in the exercise and committed to providing technical support. The consultants have completed data analysis and development of the first draft of the report, currently under review. The Steering Committee has set a goal of finalizing the evaluation by the end of November 2013.

Operations research to evaluate the sensitivity of the diagnostic algorithm is ongoing, with data collection and supervisory visits which started in January 2013. The algorithm was initially conceived with a perspective to conserve RDTs by limiting them to patients who did not have an obvious alternate cause of fever. In a context of pre-elimination, however, the identification of all parasitemic individuals becomes increasingly important, and this study is assessing the capacity of the algorithm to do so. Sixteen health facilities have been enrolled in eight districts across the country, and data collection will continue through March 2014 in order to cover both rainy and dry seasons.

Plans and Justification
At the time FY 2014 funds become available, the Senegal NMCP will be in the last year of its current strategic plan, a key moment for evaluating progress towards its pre-elimination objective and looking forward to identify and plan for the challenges ahead. Support from PMI will contribute to key data collection and analysis activities, as well as exploring issues that may hamper progress.

Proposed activities with FY 2014 funding ($1,107,000)

1. *Technical Assistance ($100,00) and Implementation of the Continuous Survey ($350,000)*
With FY 2014 resources, PMI plans to maintain its support for the continuous DHS, including TA to the National Statistics and Demography Agency to strengthen their capacity to analyze and present the data collected.

2. *Strengthening epidemiologic surveillance of malaria ($375,000)*
In response to the growing surveillance needs as Senegal moves toward pre-elimination, PMI plans to contribute to strengthening the national malaria surveillance system, including weekly case notification, in both the formal public health sector (hospitals, centers, and posts) and at the community level (health huts and home-based management). This system is expected to include electronic transmission of data by short message service (SMS) and will be integrated with the DHIS2, recently adopted by the MOH. Districts where IRS has been withdrawn will be prioritized in the pilot of weekly notification by SMS. Case investigation and active case detection are slated to be implemented where indicated. The current system includes 20 sites nationwide, but this may change as the situation evolves.

3. *Malaria program review and development of next 5 year strategic plan ($50,000)*
The 2011-2015 National Strategic Plan will be in its final year in 2015. The NMCP has requested funding to support an evaluation of the implementation and progress achieved during this five year period, as well as the development of a strategic plan for 2016-2020. Supplemental funding will be sought from other partners.

4. *Geographic information system training and software ($20,000)*
The NMCP has requested support for training on the use of geographic information system mapping applications to develop their capacity for malaria surveillance in the pre-elimination phase, particularly in relation to identifying and mapping hotspots.

6. Behavior Change Communication

NMCP/PMI Objectives
In November 2012, Senegal updated its 2008 national strategy for malaria communication to support the goals and objectives described in the 2011-2015 National Strategic Plan. This document outlines a series of challenges, objectives, and targets for the communication activities underpinning the National Strategic Plan. This communications strategy includes the following objectives:
- Increase the proportion of people sleeping under ITNs from 42% to > 80%
- Increase the proportion of pregnant women who take two doses of SP under directly observed treatment at ANC from 47% to >80%
- Increase the proportion of people who seek care at health facilities within 24 hours of the onset of fever from 45% to >80%
- Increase compliance in the treatment of uncomplicated malaria
- Increase acceptance of IRS to >90% of households in targeted districts
- Strengthen partnerships with the private sector, media, local government, Parliament and other government departments
- Monitor and evaluate the NMCP communication plan

The plan also outlines key messages, target groups, and channels through which communication activities would be carried out. These activities fall into the categories of prevention, case management, epidemic response, and communication through partnerships.

Progress since launch of PMI
PMI has supported various community mobilization and BCC activities in Senegal. These include both ongoing malaria communications (mass and interpersonal) and communication activities promoting specific events, such as IRS or LLIN distribution campaigns. Typical communications activities in Senegal have included community meetings on a specific topic, home visits, theater, community radio (radio spots as well as interviews and programming), and social mobilization (setting aside a day to focus on a specific theme or topic and bringing the whole community together around that topic – for speeches, music, skits, with banners and t-shirts with messages, etc.). Topics of ongoing IEC/BCC at community level include the importance of owning and using ITNs, prompt treatment-seeking at the health hut or health post

in the case of fever, recognition of danger signs, the importance of attending ANC visits, and the importance of receiving the recommended IPTp. Through Peace Corps Volunteers, PMI has been able to engage in malaria education and prevention throughout the country.

To date, there has been little if any effort to evaluate the impact of the different communications activities on health/malaria indicators, such as LLIN use or care seeking behavior. This weakness was voiced often as USAID/Senegal was developing its 2011-2016 health strategy and directly led to the creation of a new program to concentrate on streamlining and "upgrading" communications interventions. Going forward, the focus will be on strategic activities with specific objectives, the results of which can and will be evaluated.

Progress during the last 12 months
The NMCP, with the assistance of PMI, introduced a more strategic approach to developing and implementing communications campaigns. This approach focuses on identifying the determinants of behaviors related to malaria prevention, especially net use. From this analysis, a sustained communication campaign is developed using a mix of appropriate messages and channels. Developed with the TA of professional media/marketing firms and based on the determinants of the behaviors PMI seeks to influence, the new messages speak more personally to the targeted populations. This approach is evidence-based and measurable and will allow PMI to gauge the impact of the supported BCC campaigns.

Along these lines, the NMCP and National Health Education and Information Service (SNEIPS) created a national Malaria IEC/BCC Coordination Committee to promote harmonization of approaches and activities among the numerous partners. This was followed by a workshop to share actual materials and work plans, and to revise the 2011 malaria BCC plan. PMI supported both of these activities and has taken a lead on ensuring rigor in the development of BCC interventions. A team from Senegal, composed of the NMCP, SNEIPS, PMI and two implementing partners, attended the PMI Malaria BCC workshop in September, 2013. This provided a good opportunity to share perspectives and experience and develop a common plan for moving forward with more evidence-based communications activities.

The results of the 2012 Culture of Net Use study were used to inform BCC activities this year. For example, the study showed that many households preferred conical nets over the rectangular ones that had been distributed through the mass campaigns. Many people therefore "transformed" the nets, but the methods used often resulted in tears at the top of the nets. The NMCP and partners used interpersonal communication and demonstrations to show people ways to transform nets by using a hoop and additional fabric to reinforce the top and prevent damage. Additionally, in response to findings that some individuals do not see value in using LLINs to prevent malaria, radio spots were developed that focus on economic incentives for using nets. A radio soap opera is under development and will highlight proper net maintenance. A communications campaign was developed to accompany the introduction of subsidized LLINs in the private sector. The campaign focuses on increasing brand recognition and demand. Communications will highlight the protective qualities of the nets, their affordability, and where to obtain them.

Peace Corps Volunteers played a significant role in disseminating net transformation techniques to communities, as well as training people on care and repair techniques. Volunteers also host local language radio programs on malaria themes, help test new communications materials, and organize home visits/hang checks. Similar interpersonal communications activities were implemented through the outreach workers at health huts and sites under USAID's community health program. More than 600,000 IEC activities on different aspects of malaria control reached 1.6 million people during the year.

PMI also supported communication activities to inform potential beneficiaries about IRS and what they should expect from it, how it is beneficial to them and their family's health, and what precautions they need to take. Finally, tools to collect data on communications activities were revised and materials to support BCC activities (posters, training guides, and manuals) were produced.

Plans and Justification
With FY 2014 funds, PMI plans to support a range of communications activities to influence the social and behavior changes needed to improve the adoption of key malaria prevention and care seeking behaviors (e.g., net ownership, proper net use, net repair, when and where to seek care). Communications activities in recent years have tended to focus on LLINs due to the intensive efforts dedicated to achieving universal coverage. Now that this has been achieved, more attention can be given to other key behaviors, such as prompt care seeking, which becomes more important as transmission and acquired immunity decrease.

PMI plans to work in close partnership with the SNEIPS, NMCP, the MOH and other ministries (the Ministry of Education, Ministry of the Family, etc.), private sector entities and various other local partners. Approaches will maximize the use of effective materials/tools and media products already developed and used successfully in Senegal while also seeking to develop innovative methods. Focused on evidence-based social marketing principles, PMI plans to use a mix of channels to deliver messages that promote malaria-related products and behaviors to targeted populations. Social mobilization and mass media activities will be conducted to reach large numbers of people, while interpersonal communications will be used at the community and clinical levels to reinforce messages and tailor them to individual situations.

PMI plans to continue to promote coordination across ministries, donors, implementing partners, and the private sector to harmonize the implementation of BCC programming. PMI also plans to support qualitative and quantitative studies to identify determinates of malaria-related prevention and care-seeking behaviors. All planned BCC activities will be monitored in order to improve their outcomes and impact.

Proposed activities with FY 2014 funding ($1,775,000)

1. *Development, implementation and evaluation of BCC activities ($1,000,000)*
   PMI plans to continue to support the NMCP to implement its strategy to promote appropriate malaria prevention and care-seeking behaviors. One primary implementing partner is charged with ensuring harmonization amongst the PMI-funded partners who work at different levels of the system, from community to ministry. Support is also planned to

continue for the Malaria IEC/BCC Committee in its efforts to ensure high-quality, high-impact interventions (this committee is jointly coordinated by the NMCP and SNEIPS). PMI plans to continue working with the NMCP to engage the private sector in malaria prevention efforts. These funds are slated to be used for formative research on determinants of behavior, to contract with marketing firms to design materials and campaigns, to fund actual implementation (printing, mass media, national and regional events), and for evaluation activities.

2. *Sustaining community mobilization activities ($500,000)*
   PMI plans to continue to support a wide variety of malaria communication and education activities on LLIN use, case management, MIP and other preventive behaviors through localized community mobilization and interpersonal BCC activities. The first activity focuses primarily on strategy development and harmonization of materials, while this activity supports actual implementation at the community level by health outreach workers. Specific examples include home visits, group discussions, activities with schools, and World Malaria Day local events.

3. *Support to Peace Corps malaria related activities ($25,000)*
   Active linkages with Peace Corps Volunteers are planned to continue, allowing volunteers and their communities to benefit from the technical resources that partners provide. In this partnership, PMI benefits from the committed community presence of volunteers. Peace Corps Volunteers will also support the NMCP to implement a nationwide malaria education and prevention campaign through pre, primary, and secondary schools. Specific projects that require funding will be submitted to the Small Project Assistance committee for approval. Activities that have been funded in the past include piloting the active detection of fever cases, training women's groups/community care groups, and organizing malaria fairs.

4. *Community sensitization and mobilization for IRS ($250,000)*
   PMI plans to ensure that the targeted populations in the supported districts are appropriately informed before each spray round through radio spots, community meetings, and house-to-house visits. Information pamphlets and other materials for the household visits and social mobilization activities are slated to be updated, printed and distributed.

7. Health System Strengthening and Capacity Building

NMCP/PMI Objectives
The 2011 – 2015 National Strategic Plan identifies three key objectives for health system strengthening:
1. Ensure the availability of antimalarial drugs and products in at least 95 percent of all public and community facilities.
2. Strengthen the managerial and operational capabilities of health personnel at all levels of the health system.
3. Ensure the timeliness, completeness and use of data for M&E of the 2011-2015 National Strategic Plan.

Progress since PMI was launched

Since beginning work in Senegal, PMI has supported health system strengthening and capacity building of the MOH to implement its malaria control program. Specific interventions include pharmaceutical management activities, training, supervision, drug quality monitoring, and policy reform.

In line with GHI principles, PMI has reinforced its efforts to build capacity and integrate across programs. PMI has supported training for pharmacy managers on supply chain management as part of an integrated activity covering principles that apply to all essential drugs. Similarly, malaria drug quality monitoring was integrated with medicines for the treatment of tuberculosis and HIV/AIDS, as well as oral contraceptives, with different programs contributing to support the overall budget.

Pharmaceutical management: The ultimate goal of PMI supporting the supply chain is to ensure that SP, ACTs and RDTs are procured and made available in sufficient quantities at all service delivery points. Responding to recurrent stock outs of several commodities, PMI supported in 2011 an assessment of the CMS aimed at identifying root problems and potential solutions. Challenges included the lack of a procedures manual, inadequate utilization of the commodity management information system (e.g. tracking where different batches of a product were dispatched to), and insufficient capacity among various personnel. An action plan to implement key recommendations was developed and discussed with stakeholders. Technical assistance from PMI has also supported efforts to improve stock management at the lowest levels of the system, with an emphasis on ensuring good ACT prescribing and dispensing practices at health posts and health huts.

Capacity building: For the past several years, PMI has supported the NMCP to supervise case management at hospitals, health centers, and health posts. PMI helps build national capacity in malaria control by supporting an annual malariology course and in M&E through funding the attendance of health system staff at the annual data management and M&E course at the African Center for Advanced Management Studies (*Centre Africain des Etudes Supérieures en Gestion*). In 2012, PMI was closely involved in developing and shepherding through policy changes related to case management and prevention.

Drug quality monitoring: Since its inception, PMI has supported antimalarial drug quality monitoring by the National Drug Control Laboratory (LNCM). The nationwide network now includes nine surveillance sites and samples are collected and analyzed on an annual basis. PMI provides training, Minilab kits and supplies, and specialized TA. In particular, PMI is supporting the LNCM as it works towards International Organization for Standardization accreditation.

Progress in the last 12 months
During FY 2013, PMI continued supporting management at the CMS, particularly updating the procedures manual and improving the information management system. Integrated logistics supervision visits were conducted at all regional medical stores and health districts, and PMI also supported the NMCP to supervise case management at hospitals, health centers, and health posts.

Samples of antimalarials were collected from the nine surveillance sites around the country and tested using international quality standards. Two samples out of 327 antimalarials collected did not meet minimal quality standards and 24 were considered doubtful following the Minilab field testing (meaning more advanced testing in a lab was required to determine their quality). The proportion of suspicious drugs was slightly higher in the public sector than the private sector. PMI also supported an assessment of LNMC capacities with a view to working toward International Organization for Standardization certification. An action plan was developed based on the results and PMI continues to provide TA in specific areas.

Ten health system staff attended the annual data management and M&E course at the African Center for Advanced Management Studies

In FY 2013 PMI supported several activities aimed at improving governance of the health system for increased access and quality service delivery. The PMI funding contributed to support the implementation of the MOH's first Performance-Based Financing (PBF) experiment in three districts, with malaria prevention and case management being included in the package of services offered and for which compensation is paid. In one district, service providers were observed procuring SP from private pharmacies to provide IPTp when the stock from the CMS was not available. The first national review of this pilot has been conducted and management tools were revised. Results exceeded targets for nearly all indicators that are reimbursed under the program, including IPTp2, and expansion of the program within the pilot regions is underway. The World Bank is also providing technical and financial support for performance based financing.

Opportunities
The NMCP is fortunate to have a wealth of in-country technical capacity at its disposal, including many experienced epidemiologists, parasitologists, and entomologists who collaborate on a regular basis with the NMCP. The end of the data strike represents an opportunity to improve forecasting and quantification to reduce stock outs at the health facility and community levels.

The existence of skilled and motivated staff at the LNMC, with a vision to become an accredited reference laboratory for the sub-region, is an opportunity to improve drug quality across the health system and even in neighboring countries. The LNCM is working towards International Organization for Standardization 17025:2005 certification and can perform a wide range of drug quality controls.

Leadership changes at both the MOH and the CMS are showing signs of promise for improving supply chain management. The PMI team met with both during the MOP visit and was impressed by their commitment and motivation. The CMS Director has gone so far as to test direct delivery approaches to distant regions without warehouses using only internal resources (i.e. no outside funding or technical partners). The PMI team plans to continue to encourage MOH and CMS leadership to make the changes necessary to ensure consistent drug supplies at all levels.

Challenges
Senegal's 2011–2015 National Strategic Plan is aimed at achieving pre-elimination status by 2015. Although Senegal has a wealth of malaria prevention and control expertise at all levels, capacity building is still needed to strengthen skills for effective M&E, for applied

epidemiology, and for planning and implementing IRS activities through the government system. PMI is working with the NMCP to assist with filling the technical and leadership gap and enable the program to achieve its objectives.

Plans and Justification
The NMCP requires ongoing skills development to respond to changes in malaria trends. Increased supervision is also necessary at all levels of the health system to ensure that policies and guidelines are implemented as appropriate. Moreover, the NMCP needs continued TA from the WHO country office as the country engages in this critical pre-elimination phase. With FY2014 funding, PMI plans to support activities to develop capacity at sub-national and central levels to continue working towards the accomplishment of the NMCP's pre-elimination objective in 2015.

Proposed activities with FY 2014 funding ($1,380,000)

With FY 2014 funding, PMI plans to support the following activities to strengthen the health system and develop capacity at sub-national and central levels.

1. *Support to NMCP to enable program supervision ($175,000)*
   With FY 2014 funds, PMI plans to contribute to the NMCP's supportive supervision visits to regional and health district levels. Discussions are underway between the NMCP and its partners including PMI in order to strengthen community-level supervision as home-based delivery of integrated case management is being scaled up.

2. *State of the art capacity building opportunities ($20,000)*
   With the objective of achieving malaria pre-elimination by 2015, NMCP personnel and the country program will greatly benefit from participating in international technical, scientific and professional meetings that present opportunities to learn best practices, share experiences, and develop networks. Potential meetings include the American Society for Tropical Medicine and Hygiene and the Pan-African Malaria Conference. PMI would encourage the NMCP to seek funding from the MOH and conference organizers before supporting participation at such events.

3. *Support to NMCP to organize a malariology course ($165,000)*
   With FY 2014 funding, PMI plans to continue to support this course, enabling the participation of other categories of health system personnel beyond medical officers. The FY 2014 investment is slated to support two training sessions of 25 health professionals from district and regional health management teams(one session for senior medical officers and one for intermediate staff), with another 15 health professionals being trained through support from the Global Fund. PMI plans to revise course content to reflect the country's pre-elimination objectives.

4. *Support WHO Malaria National Professional Officer Position ($95,000)*
   PMI began funding this position in 2011 following WHO budget cuts, with the understanding that the support would be limited to two years. Unfortunately, no other funding source has been secured to maintain the position. Maintaining this position is

critical as the NMCP staff needs increased support from WHO to develop new policies and guidelines and closely monitor implementation. The Malaria National Professional Officer also serves as president of the CCM technical secretariat and his support has been pivotal in managing challenges with Global Fund disbursements and negotiations. Thus the NMCP has requested that PMI continue to support this position.

5. *Strengthening pharmaceutical management ($650,000)*
   With FY 2014 funds, PMI plans to continue to support the implementation of key reforms instituted during prior years and provide TA. PMI also plans to continue supporting the NMCP and health districts to improve quantification methods and ensure the delivery of malaria commodities. Activities will potentially include expanding the "push model" to delivery commodities directly to health facilities, which has been piloted in some areas; increasing the logistical capacity of the CMS; upgrading the information management system; and training/supervision at all levels of the supply chain.

6. *Support the NMCP for work planning and policy changes ($75,000)*
   PMI plans to continue to support the NMCP to implement the policy reforms it has undertaken, to initiate new ones as indicated, and to improve coordination among malaria partners. This will be done in the spirit of the "three ones" approach – one strategic plan, one M&E plan, and one coordination mechanism. These resources complement other, non-malaria funds dedicated to changing or implementing health policies in the country, such as the Community Health Policy that is in the works and will provide formal guidance on the roles and responsibilities of health huts. In general, these funds are slated to support staff time for the policy implementing partner as well as the organization of meetings and workshops.

7. *Drug quality monitoring and advocacy ($200,000)*
   In collaboration with the NMCP, the Directorate of Pharmacies and Medicines and the LNCM, PMI plans to continue its support to drug quality monitoring activities in nine sites. In addition, PMI plans to support advocacy for policy enforcement of drug quality standards. Proposed activities will also include TA to the LNCM as it seeks to meet the requirements to be a regional reference laboratory.

8. Staffing and Administration

Two health professionals serve as Resident Advisors to oversee the PMI in Senegal, one representing CDC and one representing USAID. In addition, one or more FSNs work as part of the PMI team. All PMI staff members are part of a single inter-agency team led by the USAID Mission Director or his/her designee in country. The PMI team shares responsibility for development and implementation of PMI strategies and work plans, coordination with national authorities, managing collaborating agencies and supervising day-to-day activities. Candidates for resident advisor positions (whether initial hires or replacements) will be evaluated and/or interviewed jointly by USAID and CDC, and both agencies will be involved in hiring decisions, with the final decision made by the individual agency.

The PMI professional staff work together to oversee all technical and administrative aspects of the PMI, including finalizing details of the project design, implementing malaria prevention and treatment activities, monitoring and evaluation of outcomes and impact, reporting of results, and providing guidance to PMI partners.

The PMI lead in country is the USAID Mission Director. The two PMI resident advisors, one from USAID and one from CDC, report to the Senior USAID Health Officer for day-to-day leadership, and work together as a part of a single interagency team. The technical expertise housed in Atlanta and Washington guides PMI programmatic efforts and thus overall technical guidance for both RAs falls to the PMI staff in Atlanta and Washington. Since CDC resident advisors are CDC employees (CDC USDD—38), responsibility for completing official performance reviews lies with the CDC Country Director who is expected to rely upon input from PMI staff across the two agencies that work closely day in and day out with the CDC RA and thus best positioned to comment on the RA's performance.

The two PMI resident advisors are based within the USAID health office and are expected to spend approximately half their time sitting with and providing technical assistance to the national malaria control programs and partners.

Locally-hired staff to support PMI activities either in Ministries or in USAID will be approved by the USAID Mission Director. Because of the need to adhere to specific country policies and USAID accounting regulations, any transfer of PMI funds directly to Ministries or host governments will need to be approved by the USAID Mission Director and Controller, in addition to the PMI Coordinator.

Proposed activities with FY 2014 funding: ($1,680,000)

These funds are slated to be used for coordination and management of all in-country PMI activities including support for salaries and benefits for two resident advisors and local staff, office equipment and supplies, and routine administration and coordination expenses.

Table 1
President's Malaria Initiative - Senegal

FY 2014 Budget Breakdown by Partner $(000)

Partner	Geographical Area	Activity	Budget ($)	%
CDC IAA	6 IRS districts	TA for entomological monitoring and operations research	$22,000	0.1%
Community Health Program Component	Nationwide	Community case management of malaria at health huts and by home-based volunteers; community mobilization for malaria prevention and treatment	$1,000,000	4.6%
DELIVER	Nationwide	Procurement of LLINs, ACTs, RDTs, SP-AQ	$6,538,000	30.3%
Health Communication and Promotion Program Component	Nationwide	Strategy development and implementation of BCC activities	$1,000,000	4.6%
Health Services Improvement Program Component	Nationwide	Strengthen MIP services; training and supervision of health service providers for malaria case management	$1,150,000	5.3%
Health System Strengthening Program Component	Nationwide	Strengthening supply chain management; support for planning and policy	$725,000	3.4%
Measure DHS	Nationwide	TA for cDHS	$100,000	0.5%
National Drug Control Laboratory	9 sites	Drug quality monitoring and advocacy	$175,000	0.8%
National Malaria Control Program	Nationwide	Implementation of routine ITN distribution system; extension of SMC strengthening malaria epidemic surveillance; program supervision; staff entomologist; malariology course	$7,185,000	33.3%
National Statistics and Demography Agency	Nationwide	Support for malaria module in cDHS	$350,000	1.6%

Partner	Geographical Area	Activity	Budget ($)	%
TBD	TBD	IRS operations; Training in mapping software	$1,020,000	4.7%
UCAD-Entomology	6 IRS districts	Entomological monitoring	$410,000	1.9%
UCAD-Parasitology	Nationwide	Therapeutic efficacy testing	$100,000	0.5%
US Peace Corps	Nationwide	Support to Peace Corps malaria activities	$25,000	0.1%
US Pharmacopeia	Nationwide	TA for accreditation and drug quality monitoring	$25,000	0.1%
WHO Umbrella Grant		Support for malaria National Professional Officer	$95,000	0.4%
CDC/USAID	Nationwide	In-country staffing and administration	$1,680,000	7.8%
Total			**$21,600,000**	**100%**

Table 2
President's Malaria Initiative – Senegal
Planned Malaria Obligations for FY 2014, Breakdown by Activity

Proposed Activity	Mechanism	Budget		Geographic Area	Description
		Total $	Commodity $		
PREVENTIVE ACTIVITIES					
Insecticide-Treated Nets					
Procurement and distribution of LLINs for distribution through campaigns and routine	DELIVER	4,000,000	4,000,000	Nationwide	1,000,000 LLINs primarily for distribution through routine channels
Operational costs of maintaining routine distribution system and for mass distribution	NMCP	800,000		Nationwide	Transport, coupons, supervision
SUBTOTAL ITNs		**4,800,000**	**4,000,000**		
Indoor Residual Spraying					
IRS operations	TBD	1,000,000		4 districts	TA
	NMCP	3,800,000	2,000,000	4 districts	Assumes transfer of majority of operational costs to NMCP. Exact funding breakdown TBD.
Entomological monitoring	UCAD-Ento	410,000		Nationwide	Entomologic monitoring post IRS implementation and following UC of LLINs, exact districts TBD
	CDC IAA	22,000		N/A	$12,000 TA, $10,000 supplies
SUBTOTAL IRS		**5,232,000**	**2,000,000**		
Malaria in Pregnancy					

Proposed Activity	Mechanism	Budget		Geographic Area	Description
		Total $	Commodity $		
Reinforce provision of effective MIP services in health facilities and in outreach strategies	Health Services Improvement Program Component	600,000		Nationwide	Monitoring and supportive supervision, update materials to reflect revised guidelines, training of new staff. Cups and water filters as needed for directly-observed treatment with SP.
SUBTOTAL MIP		**600,000**			
SUBTOTAL PREVENTIVE		**10,632,000**	**6,000,000**		
CASE MANAGEMENT					
Diagnosis					
Strengthening microscopic diagnosis of malaria	NMCP	200,000		Nationwide	Conduct supervision for quality assurance and quality control of microscopy and RDTs
Microscopes and lab consumables	DELIVER	50,000	50,000	Nationwide	15 microscopes
Procurement of RDTs	DELIVER	1,396,000	1,396,000	Nationwide	2.25 million RDTs to cover country's needs
SUBTOTAL DIAGNOSIS		**1,646,000**	**1,446,000**		
Treatment					
Improve case management of malaria	Health Services Improvement project	550,000		Nationwide	Support for training and supervision of case management of malaria at all levels of the health system, including the private sector

Proposed Activity	Mechanism	Budget		Geographic Area	Description
		Total $	Commodity $		
Community case management of malaria with ACTs and diagnosis with RDTs	Community Health Program Component	500,000		Nationwide	Community based case management of fever as part of an integrated package of services in more than 2,000 functional health huts. Includes training, supervision, and monitoring of staff.
Supervision of integrated PECADOM program	NMCP	450,000		Selected districts	Supervision of DSDOMs recently trained in integrated package
Procure ACTs	DELIVER	525,000	525,000	Nationwide	ASAQ for most of the country, AL for 4 SMC regions.
Implementation of SMC	NMCP	900,000		Kedougou, Sedhiou, Kolda, Tambacounda	Monthly doses of SP-AQ provided by community volunteers in campaigns for 3-4 months during transmission season. Will cover approx. 600,000 children 3-120 months of age.
Procurement of drugs for SMC	DELIVER	542,000	330,000		Procure and distribute rectal artesunate for pre-referral treatment of severe malaria
Procurement of drugs for pre-referral treatment	DELIVER	25,000	25,000		
Therapeutic efficacy studies	UCAD-Parasitology	100,000			Includes monitoring resistance markers for SP-AQ in SMC regions. Rotation every 2 years among 4 sites (2 sites per year).
SUBTOTAL TREATMENT		3,592,000	880,000		
SUBTOTAL CASE MANAGEMENT		5,238,000	2,326,000		

48

Proposed Activity	Mechanism	Budget		Geographic Area	Description
		Total $	Commodity $		
MONITORING AND EVALUATION/OPERATIONS RESEARCH					
TA for the cDHS	Measure DHS	100,000			Technical assistance for sampling and analysis
Support to malaria module in cDHS	National Statistics and Demography Agency	350,000		Nationwide	Operational support to a full malaria module as part of cDHS, including biomarkers. Co-funding from other donors.
Strengthening malaria surveillance and response	NMCP	375,000		Nationwide	Strengthening notification, particularly using mobile communication. Perhaps addition of sites. Funds reserved for potential response to epidemics ($75,000).
Malaria program review and development of National Strategic Plan	NMCP	50,000			Evaluation of 2011-2015 plan and development of 2016-2020 plan
Training/TA for mapping; purchase necessary software	TBD	20,000			To aid decision making, documentation. Better visibility of "hot spots".
SUBTOTAL M&E / OR		1,107,000	0		
BEHAVIOR CHANGE COMMUNICATION					
Development, implementation and evaluation of BCC activities	Health Communications and Promotion	1,000,000			???

Proposed Activity	Mechanism	Budget		Geographic Area	Description
		Total $	Commodity $		
Sustaining community mobilization activities	Community Health Program Component	500,000		Nationwide	Comprehensive malaria community mobilization activities including IEC/BCC, support for MIP, case management, ITNs
Support to Peace Corps malaria related activities	Small Projects Assistance Peace Corps	25,000		Peace Corps Volunteer communities	
Community sensitization and mobilization for IRS	NMCP	250,000		4 districts	
SUBTOTAL BCC		1,775,000	0		
HEALTH SYSTEM STRENGTHENING / CAPACITY BUILDING					
Support to NMCP to enable program supervision	NMCP	175,000		Nationwide	Support visits by national staff to regional and district levels
State of the art capacity building opportunities	NMCP	20,000			ASTMH, MIM. 2 trips, 2 people each.
Support for malariology course of the NMCP	NMCP	165,000		N/A	Malariology course for district and regional staff, content adapted for pre-elimination context. Co-funding from Global Fund under Phase 2. 1 cadre superieur, 1 cadre intermediaire. 25 people per session.
Support WHO National Malaria Professional Officer	WHO Umbrella Grant	95,000			

Proposed Activity	Mechanism	Budget		Geographic Area	Description
		Total $	Commodity $		
Supply chain management and drug management strengthening	Health System Strengthening Program Component	650,000		Nationwide	Follow-up on reforms instituted prior year, TA
Support for planning and policy reforms related to malaria	Health System Strengthening Program Component	75,000			support to NMCP for work planning, policy changes
Drug quality monitoring and advocacy	National Drug Control Laboratory	175,000		Nationwide	Sampling and testing antimalarials from 9 sites nationwide.
	USP	25,000			TA for accreditation and drug quality monitoring.
SUBTOTAL HSS & CAPACITY BUILDING		**1,380,000**	**0**		
IN-COUNTRY STAFFING AND ADMINISTRATION					
In-country staff Administrative expenses	CDC/USAID	1,680,000		Nationwide	Coordination of all in-country PMI activities
SUBTOTAL IN-COUNTRY STAFFING		**1,680,000**	**0**		
GRAND TOTAL		**21,600,000**	**8,326,000**		

References

1. Human Development Report 2013: Senegal. Available on web at http://hdrstats.undp.org/en/countries/profiles/SEN.html. Accessed 14 May 2013.

2. L'Agence Nationale du Statistique and ICF International. 2012. 2010-11 Senegal Demographic and Health and Multiple Indicators Survey: Key Findings. Calverton, Maryland, USA: ANSD and ICF International.

3. UNAIDS/WHO Global report: UNAIDS Report on the Global AIDS Epidemic 2010. Available on web at http://www.unaids.org/documents/20101123_GlobalReport_Annexes1_em.pdf. Accessed 14 May 2013.

4. Ndiaye, S, Ayad, M. 2006. 2005 Senegal Demographic and Health Survey (DHS). Calverton, Maryland USA: Centre de recherche pour le développement humain (Sénégal) and ORC Macro

5. Ndiaye, Salif, and Mohamed Ayad. 2007. Senegal Malaria Indicator Survey 2006. Calverton, Maryland, USA : Centre de Recherche pour le Développement Humain [Sénégal] and Macro International Inc.

6. Ndiaye, S. et al. 2009. 2008/9 Senegal Malaria Indicator Survey. Calverton, Maryland USA: Centre de Recherche pour le développement humain (Sénégal) and ORC Macro.

7. Programme National de Lutte Contre le Paludisme. 2010. Evaluation de la campagne intégrée de distribution de moustiquaires imprégnées à longue durée d'action, de vitamine A, et de mébendazole au Sénégal 2009.

8. Tine RC, Faye B, Ndour CT, Ndiaye JL, Ndiaye M, Bassene C, Magnussen P, Bygbjerg IC, Sylla K. Impact of combining intermittent preventive treatment with home management of malaria in children less than 10 years in a rural area of Senegal: a cluster randomized trial. Malar J. 2011 Dec 13;10:358. doi: 10.1186/1475-2875-10-358.

www.ingramcontent.com/pod-product-compliance
Lightning Source LLC
Chambersburg PA
CBHW080612290526
45790CB00007B/2742